Literacy in Action

Authors

Dr. Sharon Jeroski

Andrea Bishop
Jean Bowman
Lynn Bryan
Linda Charko
Maureen Dockendorf
Christine Finochio
Jo Ann Grime
Joanne Leblanc-Haley
Deidre McConnell
Carol Munro
Cathie Peters
Lorraine Prokopchuk
Arnold Toutant

PEARSON

Education
Canada

Grade 5 Project Team

Team Leader and Publisher: Anita Borovilos
National Literacy Consultants: Beth Ecclestone and Norma MacFarlane
Publishers: Susan Green and Elynor Kagan
Product Manager: Donna Neumann
Managing Editor: Monica Schwalbe
Developmental Editors: Amanjeet Chauhan, Elaine Gareau, Su Mei Ku, and Anne MacInnes
Production Editors: Amanjeet Chauhan and Adele Reynolds
Copy Editors: Lisa Santilli, Rebecca Vogan, and Jessica Westhead
Research: Nancy Belle Cook and Glen Herbert
Production Coordinators: Donna Brown and Zane Kaneps
Senior Manufacturing Coordinator: Jane Schell
Art Director: Zena Denchik
Designers: Zena Denchik, Maki Ikushima, Carolyn Sebestyen, Sonya V. Thursby/Opus House Inc., and Word & Image Design
Permissions Research: Cindy Howard
Photo Research: Nancy Belle Cook, Glen Herbert, Cindy Howard, and Terri Rothman
Vice-President Publishing and Marketing: Mark Cobham

ISBN-13: 978-0-13-204719-7 (softcover)
ISBN-10: 0-13-204719-5 (softcover)
ISBN13: 978-0-13-204718-0 (hardcover)
ISBN-10: 0-13-204718-7 (hardcover)

Printed and bound in Canada.
1 2 3 4 5 TC 11 10 09 08 07

The publisher has taken every care to meet or exceed industry specifications for the manufacture of textbooks. The cover of this sewn book is a premium, polymer-reinforced material designed to provide long life and withstand rugged use. Mylar gloss lamination has been applied for further durability.

PEARSON
Education
Canada

Acknowledgements

Series Consultants

Andrea Bishop
Anne Boyd
Christine Finochio
Don Jones
Joanne Leblanc-Haley
Jill Maar
Joanne Rowlandson
Carole Stickley

Specialist Reviewers

Science: Doug Herridge
  Toronto, ON
Social Studies: Marg Lysecki
  Toronto, ON
Aboriginal: Ken Ealey
  Edmonton, AB

Equity: Dianna Mezzarobba
  Vancouver, BC
Levelling: Susan Pleli
  Stoney Creek, ON
Iris Zammit
  Toronto, ON

Grades 3–6 Advisors and Reviewers

Dr. Frank Serafini
  Assistant Professor,
  University of Las Vegas,
  Las Vegas, Nevada

Patricia Adamson
  Winnipeg, MB
Marion Ahrens
  Richmond Hill, ON
Sandra Ball
  Surrey, BC
Gwen Bartnik
  Vancouver, BC
Jennifer Batycky
  Calgary, AB
Michelle Bellavia
  Hamilton, ON
Mary-Jane Black
  Hamilton, ON
Jackie Bradley
  Saskatoon, SK
Diane Campbell
  Durham, ON
Nancy Carl
  Coquitlam, BC
Janet Chow
  Burnaby, BC
Marla Ciccotelli
  London, ON
Susan Clarke
  Burlington, ON
Norma Collinson
  Truro, NS
Lynn Crews
  Lower Sackville, NS
Kathryn D'Angelo
  Richmond, BC

Susan Elliott
  Toronto, ON
Diane Gagley
  Calgary, AB
Michael Gallant
  Calgary, AB
Jennifer Gardner
  Vernon, BC
Adrienne Gear
  Vancouver, BC
Faye Gertz
  Niska, AB
Cindy Gordon
  Victoria, BC
James Gray
  Winnipeg, MB
Kathleen Gregory
  Victoria, BC
Myrtis Guy
  Torbay, NL
Kim Guyette-Carter
  Dartmouth, NS
Jackie Hall
  Vancouver, BC
Natalie Harnum
  Berwick, NS
Sherida Hassanali
  Herring Cove, NS
Deborah Holley
  Duncan, BC
Joanne Holme
  Surrey, BC
Patricia Horstead
  Maple Ridge, BC
Carol Hryniuk-Adamov
  Winnipeg, MB
Pamela Jacob
  Limestone, ON

Joanne Keller
  Delta, BC
Dawn Kesslering
  Regina, SK
Karen Quan King
  Toronto, ON
Linda Kirby
  Sault Ste. Marie, ON
Sheryl Koers
  Duncan, BC
Roger Lacey
  Calgary, AB
Sharon LeClair
  Coquitlam, BC
Caroline Lutyk
  Burlington, ON
Heather MacKay
  Richmond, BC
Margaret Marion
  Niagara Falls, ON
Sangeeta McAuley
  Toronto, ON
Paula McIntee
  Allanburg, ON
Caroline Mitchell
  Guelph, ON
Laura Mossey
  Durham, ON
Rhonda Nixon
  Edmonton, AB
Gillian Parsons
  Brantford, ON
Linda Perrin
  Saint John, NB
Charolette Player
  Edmonton, AB
Rhonda Rakimov
  Duncan, BC

Tammy Renyard
  Duncan, BC
Kristine Richards
  Windsor, ON
Kathryn Richmond
  St. Catharines, ON
Barbara Rushton
  New Minas, NS
Jaye Sawatsky
  Delta, BC
Michelle Sharratt
  Woodbridge, ON
Cathy Sheridan
  Ottawa, ON
Nanci-Jane Simpson
  Hamilton, ON
Kim Smith
  Newmarket, ON
Candace Spilsbury
  Duncan, BC
Sheila Staats
  Brantford, ON
Patricia Tapp
  Hamilton, ON
Vera Teschow
  Mississauga, ON
Joanne Traczuk
  Sutton West, ON
Sonja Willier
  Edmonton, AB
Susan Wilson
  St. Catharines, ON
Kelly Winney
  London, ON
Beth Zimmerman
  London, ON

CONTENTS

UNIT 1

It's About Respect • 2

Read Together

. . . .

Showing Respect • 4
   (questionnaire)

Shared

. . . .

Learn Together Poster

Guided Practice

. . . .

Profiles of Respect
   by Sheila Fletcher (biographies)

Todd Wong • 10

Viola Irene Desmond • 12

Erica Samms-Hurley • 14

Literacy in Action

Reading Biographies .8

Think Like a Reader .9

Reflect on Your Reading 16

Read Like a Writer .17

Independent Practice

For the Love of the Game • 18
  by the Canadian Baseball Hall of Fame
  (Internet article)

Speaking Out for Children's Rights • 23
  by Craig Kielburger (autobiography)

Read! Write! Say! Do!

Images of Respect • 28
  (murals)

Faces • 32
  (self-portraits)

There Is No They, Only Us • 34
  by Monique White Butterfly (poem)

The Language of Friendship • 38
  by Tori Schnoor (narrative non-fiction)

My Gran's Different • 40
  by Sue Lawson and Caroline Magerl
  (narrative poem)

Going with the Flow • 46
  by Claire H. Blatchford (narrative fiction)

Your Literacy Portfolio

Producers at Work! 36
Connect and Share 60
Spotlight on Learning 61

Hooked on Ads • 62

View Together

Ad Smart • 64
  by Peter (magazine article)

Shared

Learn Together Poster

Guided Practice

The Big Sell
  (graphic stories)

Better Than Being There! • 70

Be a Winner! • 72

Wired Sounds! • 74

Literacy in Action

Viewing Advertisements 68

Think Like a Viewer 69

Reflect on Your Viewing 76

View Like an Advertiser 77

Independent Practice

You Are the Target! • 78
   by Su Mei Ku (report)

Food Tricks You Should Know About! • 82
   by PBS Kids (Internet article)

Read! Write! Say! Do!

Truth in Advertising? • 85
   by Liam O'Donnell (graphic story)

What's Next? • 90
   by Esther Fleming (report)

Online Marketing Strategies • 92
   by the Media Awareness Network
   (Internet article)

Ads: They're Not *All* Bad! • 97
   by Allan Badali (public service ads)

Sidewalk Circus • 104
   by Paul Fleischman and Kevin Hawkes
   (graphic story)

The Kid from the Commercial • 110
   adapted by Aaron Shepard from the
   book by Stephen Manes (play)

Your Literacy Portfolio

Advertisers at Work! 102
Connect and Share .118
Spotlight on Learning 119

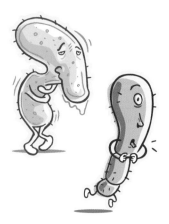

UNIT 3

Body Works • 120

Read Together

Wash Up • 122
by Mandy Ng (magazine article)

Shared

Learn Together Poster

Guided Practice

Body Organs
by Sheila Fletcher (explanations)

Your Heart • 128

Your Lungs • 130

Your Skin • 132

Literacy in Action

Reading in Science 126

Think Like a Reader 127

Reflect on Your Reading 134

Read Like a Writer 135

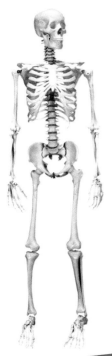

Independent Practice

Let's Get Moving! • 136
    by Jane Bingham (explanation)

Your Eyes, Your Voice, Even Your Smell:
Your New ID • 141
    by Rick Book (explanation)

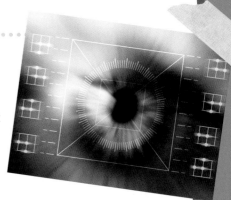

Read! Write! Say! Do!

How to Eat Like a Cat • 146
    by Nick D'Alto (play/procedural)

Body Verse • 154
    by Jon Scieszka (poems)

Hidden Worlds Magnified • 157
    (photographs)

By the Numbers: Fun Facts About
Our Bodies • 161
    by Rachel Proud (information)

How Do You Rate *Your* Health? • 164
    by Daniel Girard (newspaper article)

The Buffalo Bull and the Cedar Tree • 168
    by Joseph Bruchac (legend)

Smog City • 172
    by Chris Butler (short story)

Your Literacy Portfolio

Researchers at Work! .152
Connect and Share 178
Spotlight on Learning .179

It's About Respect

LEARNING GOALS

In this unit you will

- Read, listen to, and view biographic information.

- Contribute to and work together in groups.

- Make connections to your own life and other selections.

- Create presentations about respect.

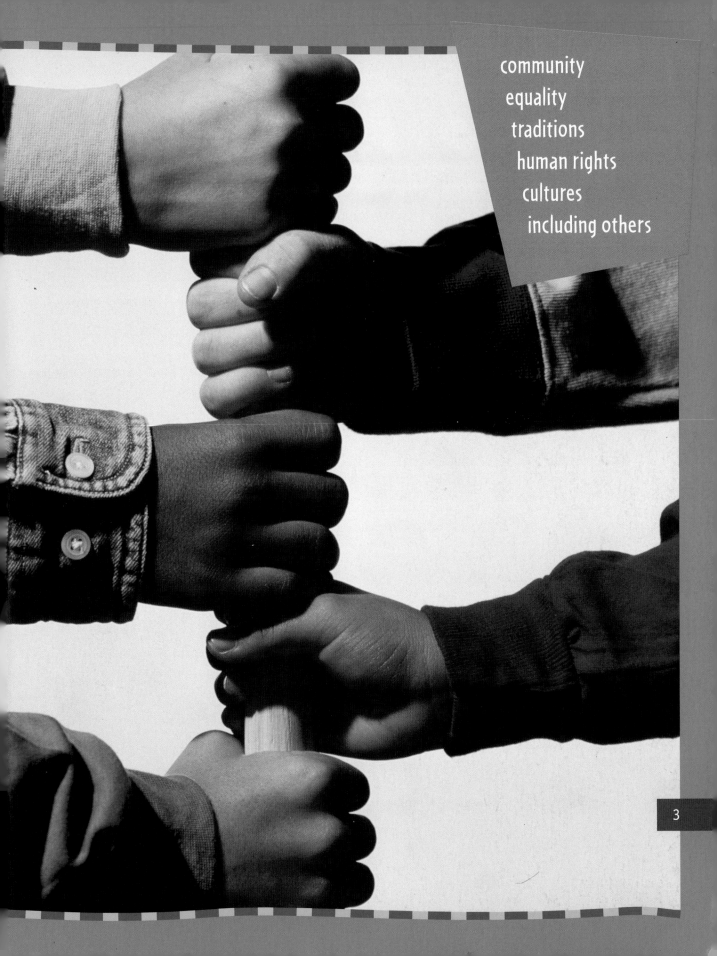

community
equality
traditions
human rights
cultures
including others

3

showing Respect

How do people show respect?

Questionnaires can tell us a lot about what people think. As you read the questionnaire on the next page together, think about how you might respond to each question. Then turn the page and see how some people answered other questions about respect.

Every human being, of whatever origin, of whatever station, deserves respect.
—U Thant, former Secretary General of the United Nations

A Questionnaire for You

Q.1

Do you try to make sure others feel included? How?

Q.2

Have you ever stood up for someone who wasn't being treated with respect? If so, what did you do?

Q.3

Do you enjoy learning about cultures and languages that are different from your own? Why?

Q.4

Do you ever try to put yourself in someone else's shoes? How does it feel?

Q.5

Do you treat others the way you would like to be treated? Why?

Q.6

Do you accept ways that others are different? How?

Q.7

Do you respect the belongings of others? How?

Q.8

Do you help to look after your home? Your school? Your community? In what ways?

Q.9

What does showing respect mean to you?

A Community Survey

What do people think about respect in their communities?

A survey is another way we can find out what people think. Interviewers asked 1000 adults some key questions about respect in their communities. The graphs on the next page show what they found out.

No act of kindness, no matter how small, is ever wasted.
—Aesop, Greek fable author

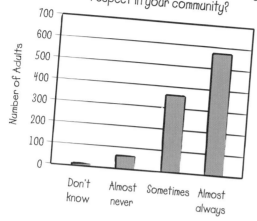

How often do you see people showing respect in your community?

(Bar graph — Number of Adults vs. Don't know, Almost never, Sometimes, Almost always)

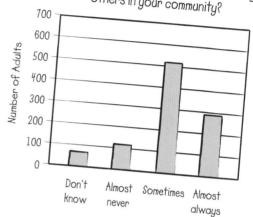

How often do you see people including others in your community?

(Bar graph — Number of Adults vs. Don't know, Almost never, Sometimes, Almost always)

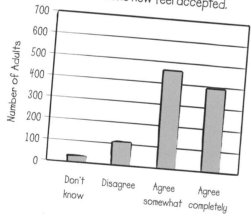

People in our community would help someone new feel accepted.

(Bar graph — Number of Adults vs. Don't know, Disagree, Agree somewhat, Agree completely)

LET'S TALK ABOUT IT...

- Choose one of the questions on page 5. Role-play a situation to show what respect looks and sounds like.

- For the community survey, the interviewers spoke to adults. What do you think the results would be if you asked students in your school the same questions?

Reading Biographies

Biographies give information about people's lives. Some biographies tell a person's whole life story. Others give just a few highlights.

TALK ABOUT IT!

- Talk to a partner or group about a biography you have read or viewed.
- Whose life story was it?
- Why do you think this person was chosen for a biography?
- What made this person's life interesting?

You can find biographies and biographic profiles in many places. Here are some hints!

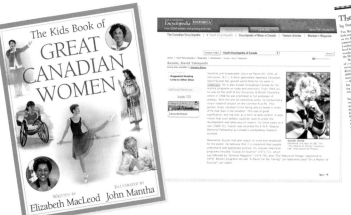

Make a table listing the kinds of people who are featured in biographies. Note why you are interested in their lives.

People	Why they are interesting
Explorers	Their lives are often dangerous and exciting.
Athletes	They train hard to achieve their goals.

Think Like a Reader

autobiography
accomplishment
obstacle

Read with a purpose

- Why do you read biographies?

Crack the code

Here are some words that can help you read and write biographies. What strategies can help you read these words?

Make meaning

Practise using these strategies when you read biographies:

PREDICT   Look at the headings and pictures for clues. What do you predict this selection will be about?

PAUSE AND CHECK   As you read, think about your predictions. Were you right? Make new predictions about what you will read.

CONNECT   Think about how the biography relates to your own life or to the lives of other people you know or know about.

Analyze what you read

- Why do you think people write biographies?
- How might two writers tell the same person's life story in different ways?

Todd Wong

Born: May 11, 1960

Home: Vancouver, BC

Work: Vancouver Public Library

His Words:

" This is what Canadian society is all about, introducing each other to our cultures and welcoming other cultures into our families."

Todd in a Scottish kilt

A New Idea

Gung Haggis Fat Choy. What do you think that is? It sounds like *Gung Hei Fat Choy*, which is what many people say to each other to celebrate the Chinese New Year. But haggis is the national dish of Scotland! To understand Gung Haggis Fat Choy, you need to meet Todd Wong. It was all his idea.

Todd Wong is a Chinese Canadian whose family has lived in BC since the 1800s. In 1993, Todd was a student at Simon Fraser University in Burnaby, BC. On January 25, Robbie Burns Day was to be celebrated. On that date each year, people of Scottish origin celebrate the life of their national poet, Robert Burns. Todd was asked to help with the celebration, but he said no. He just couldn't picture himself dressed in a Scottish kilt. It was too weird! But no one else would volunteer, so Todd finally agreed. This was the start of something big!

What a Party!

Now, let's go back to Gung Haggis Fat Choy. In 1998, Chinese New Year and Robbie Burns Day were only two days apart. Todd planned to cook a Chinese New Year's dinner for some friends. Why not combine the celebration with Robbie Burns Day? he thought. And so the Gung Haggis Fat Choy dinner began. For that day, Todd would be known as Toddish McWong. To entertain his guests, he would play Scottish songs on his accordion. He would read poetry by Asian Canadians and Robbie Burns.

That party was a great success. The next year's party was an even greater success. In following years, more and more people attended. There are now hundreds of guests and everyone enjoys delicious food and great entertainment. The money raised goes to projects such as the Asian Canadian Writers' Workshop. Todd has been heard on radio across Canada and in Scotland. One simple idea has touched so many people.

PAUSE AND CHECK
What might happen at a Gung Haggis Fat Choy party?

CONNECT
How does Todd remind you of other people you know or know about?

Todd Wong also participates in the dragon boat races. The event is another way people of different cultures can celebrate together.

Viola Irene Desmond

Born: July 6, 1914

Home: Halifax, NS

Died: February 7, 1965

Her Words:

"You must remain who you are and what you are, and as our parents taught us, be proud of yourself."

Viola in the 1940s

A Life-Changing Event

PREDICT,

How do you think Viola Desmond might represent respect?

Viola Desmond came from a well-known African Canadian family in Halifax, Nova Scotia. She owned a beauty salon and school. On November 9, 1946, her quiet life changed when she went on a business trip from Halifax to Sydney. As she drove through New Glasgow, she had car trouble. She left the car at a garage and found a place to stay. She then wondered how to pass the time. In those days, there were no television sets or video games, so she went to a movie theatre.

Since Viola had trouble seeing things from a distance, she sat downstairs in the theatre, quite close to the screen. Just as she settled in, an usher told her to move upstairs because the downstairs seats cost more. When she offered to pay, the usher told her she couldn't pay—she just had to move.

12

There was no sign that said only White people could sit downstairs, but Viola knew that was the reason. She stayed where she was. Soon, the police came and dragged her out of the theatre. She was put in jail, where she sat all night on a hard bench.

PAUSE AND CHECK

How might Viola's actions change the way people are treated?

An Issue of Respect

Next day, she was charged with trying to cheat the government since the downstairs seat cost more than the upstairs one. The extra cost was only one cent more. When Viola tried to explain that she had offered to buy a ticket for the downstairs seat, the judge ignored her. He said she must pay a $20 fine.

A human rights group in Halifax paid her fine, but Viola did not stop there. She asked the group to help her appeal the judge's decision. It wasn't easy. Some people felt there were other more important issues for African Canadians at that time. The group made many appeals and lost them all, but people took note of Viola's actions. In 1954, Nova Scotia passed laws against separating people because of their skin colour.

Viola (left) with her sister Wanda Robson in 1955.

CONNECT

How does Viola remind you of other people you know or know about?

13

Erica Samms-Hurley

Born: November 4, 1981

Home: Mount Moriah, NL

Member: Elmastogoeg First Nation (Benoit's Cove Band)

Her Words:

"I think about all the other young Aboriginal women out there, working just as hard and harder than I am, fighting for equality in Canada."

Erica at home in Newfoundland and Labrador

PREDICT

How do you think Erica Samms-Hurley might represent respect?

An Award Winner

At the age of 24, Erica Samms-Hurley received something special. She was awarded the Governor General's Youth Award for her work in health care. As a registered nurse, Erica has worked to promote health care among Aboriginal peoples, especially women and youth.

Working in health care has been important to Erica since she was young. She says, "I was probably 15 or 16 years old when my grandfather became very ill. As I watched my mother care for him, the whole nursing aspect really touched me. I think from then on, I knew I wanted to do something in the medical profession."

Working for Change

Erica is a Mi'kmaw from Newfoundland and Labrador. She learned from her parents and grandparents about the history and traditions of her people. At school, she sometimes had to deal with others who did not respect her or her people's traditions. "Other people were quick to make fun of things they knew little about," she says. "So, I denied myself the right to be proud of who I was. Later, I learned how to fight against life's barriers. I learned how to use the voice I was given. I started working with other Aboriginal youth. By sharing my story I hoped that others would not feel alone when they dealt with issues such as the ones I dealt with."

As she talks about her award, Erica says, "I will never forget the moment when the Governor General placed the award around my neck. She said, 'I am sure we will be seeing each other again in the near future. I wish you the best.' The proud look on my family's faces was something pictures could not capture."

PAUSE AND CHECK

How might Erica continue her work for Aboriginal people?

CONNECT

How does Erica remind you of other people you know or know about?

The award Erica received from Governor General Michaëlle Jean goes to people who are working to improve the lives of women.

15

Reflect on Your Reading

You have . . .

- talked about respect.
- read about people who tried to make sure everyone is treated with respect.
- explored words and phrases related to respect and to biographies.

equality   caring

feeling proud

community

sharing

I think it is important to stand up for myself and others. What do you think?

You have also . . .

- explored different reading strategies.

PREDICT
PAUSE AND CHECK
CONNECT

Write About Learning

Write about one of the strategies you used when you read the selection "Profiles of Respect." How did the strategy help you read and understand the person's life and accomplishments? Tell how the strategy might help you when you read other biographies.

Read Like a Writer

When you were reading "Profiles of Respect," you were reading biographies.

TALK ABOUT IT!

- What do you notice about the way biographies are written?

- How are they different from fictional stories?

- How are they different from other kinds of information?

- Make a chart showing what you notice about how biographies are organized.

HINT!

Look at how the information is **organized**.

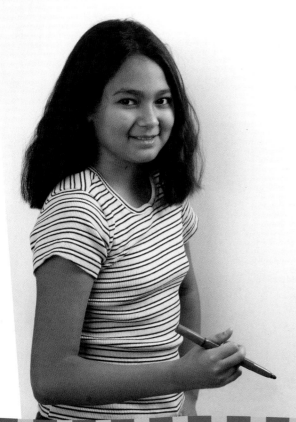

Biographies: Organization
- have an interesting beginning
- tell events in order
- use words like <u>next</u>, <u>after</u>, and <u>in 1922</u> to show when or in what order events happened

For the Love of THE GAME

Why have some people had to wait for respect?

A Remarkable Team

This is a story that began in 1914, but the happy ending had to wait until 2003! It's a story about a baseball team whose players earned respect and admiration wherever they played.

The baseball team was called Asahi, and the players were Japanese Canadians. The team was the pride of Vancouver's Japanese community. Hopeful players (some as young as eight years of age) came from Vancouver and nearby towns, villages, and farms to try out for the team. Wearing the Asahi uniform became the dream of many Japanese Canadian boys.

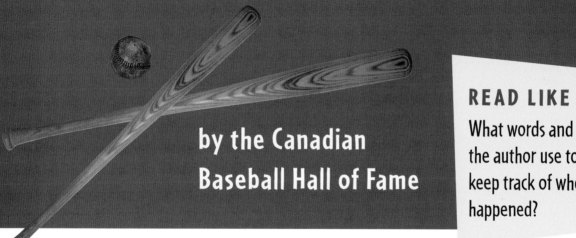

by the Canadian Baseball Hall of Fame

READ LIKE A WRITER

What words and phrases does the author use to help readers keep track of when events happened?

The Asahi players were so fast that they could steal bases without getting caught—and they stole a lot of them! They placed bunts with amazing accuracy. They were hard to beat. People called the Asahi type of baseball game "brain ball."

History

By the 1930s, the Asahi team was playing in Vancouver's Senior City League. It was the only Japanese Canadian team in the league. The players were so good that everyone on the West Coast wanted to see them play. Beginning in 1937, Asahi won the famous Pacific Northwest Championship five years in a row.

"The players won the hearts and respect of the fans with their brilliant fielding, pitching, and spectacular base running." Japanese Canadian Association

But World War II changed everything for the Asahi players. The summer of 1941 would be their last carefree season. Japan attacked Pearl Harbor in December of 1941. Soon after, the Canadian government sent all people of Japanese descent to prison camps called internment camps. The government also took away their homes and their belongings.

The Asahi players were sent to different camps all across British Columbia. Although they never played ball as a team again, each player took with him the spirit of the game. Even in this new hard life, baseball slowly crept in. Little by little, bats and balls appeared. The Asahi players began to play baseball again, putting together teams in camps throughout the province.

When Japan bombed Pearl Harbor in 1941, the Canadian government declared war against Japan. Japanese Canadians were sent to internment camps even though many of them had been born in Canada and were Canadian citizens.

20

My Asahi Notebook

Ken Kutsukake was 12 years old when he started playing with the Asahi team. He was a great catcher, and his nickname was "Catcha-catcha-Kutsukake"! He formed a team in the Kaslo internment camp with pitcher Naggie Nishihara. When Ken was released in 1947, he joined the Atwater Baseball Team in Montreal. He moved to Toronto in 1948, where he played at Christie Pits. He coached in several divisions and was a huge Blue Jays fan.

Kiyoshi Suga started as a bat boy for the Asahi in 1932. His two older brothers played on the team, and three uncles worked in the Asahi organization. While he was in an internment camp, he played on the Lemon Creek All-Stars. When he was set free, he moved to Vernon, British Columbia, to play for the Okanagan Valley Senior League. He then moved to Montreal, where he became a catcher for the Montreal Niseis.

Asahi: A Timeline

1914 Asahi Baseball Club forms. (Asahi means Morning Sun.)

1926 The club becomes the first Japanese Canadian team to win the Terminal League championship.

1937 Asahi wins the Pacific Northwest Championship. The team then wins it five years in a row.

1941 The club disbands because the players are sent to internment camps.

2003 Asahi is inducted into the Canadian Baseball Hall of Fame.

2005 The club is inducted into the BC Sports Hall of Fame.

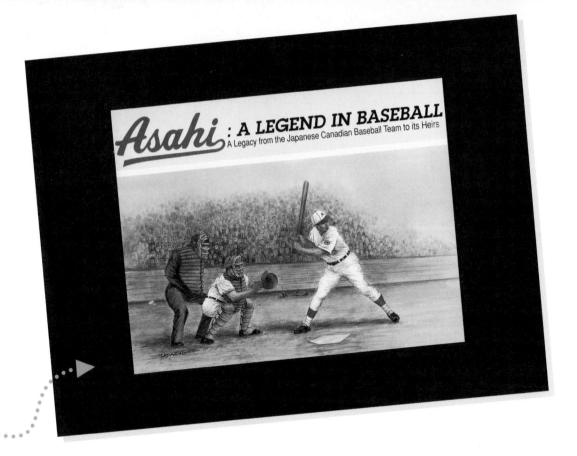

Asahi : A LEGEND IN BASEBALL
A Legacy from the Japanese Canadian Baseball Team to its Heirs

TADACHI

Author Pat Adachi's father started taking her to Asahi games when she was eight years old. She wrote a book to show how much the Asahi baseball team meant to people.

New Beginnings

Soon the Japanese Canadians in the camps began playing baseball with their RCMP guards. Then people from the local towns wanted to join in. Many of them had never seen a Japanese person before, and they were surprised to hear the players speak perfect English. Baseball became a common bond between the two groups. It helped the townspeople to lose their suspicion and fear of Japanese Canadians, and it led to lasting friendships that continue today.

DIG DEEPER

1. Role-play a radio interview with one of the players or fans.
2. Research to find information about the internment of Japanese Canadians. Write a short biography of one person you learn about.

Speaking Out for Children's Rights
by Craig Kielburger

Why is it important to care for people in other places?

Beginnings

My journey as a child rights activist began on an ordinary Wednesday morning when I was 12. Sitting at the breakfast table, I was flipping through the paper toward the comics when a headline jumped out at me: "Battled child labour, boy, 12, murdered."

Curious, I sat down to read the article. That's when I first learned about the life and death of Iqbal Masih, a former child labourer who became a child rights activist. Sold into slavery at the age of four, this Pakistani boy spent six years chained to a carpet-weaving loom. He escaped and spoke out for the rights of enslaved children. His calls for justice captured the world's attention. They also probably led a carpet-maker to have him killed.

Iqbal's story shocked me. Iqbal and I were the same age, but our lives were so different. Of course, I'd seen suffering on TV, in the newspaper, and even walking past homeless people. But like most others, I'd learned to tune it out. Reading Iqbal's story changed that. I was angry.

READ LIKE A WRITER
What does the writer do to catch your interest in the first sentence?

23

Craig and his friends started Free The Children to raise awareness about child labour around the world.

Taking Action

I headed to the library to learn more, and that's when I made another terrible discovery: In many parts of the world, instead of going to school, children exactly like me were forced to work in the most awful conditions. It seemed unbelievable that I'd never heard about any of this before. Was I the only one?

I decided to share what I'd learned with my class. I felt nervous standing in front of my classmates, telling them about Iqbal and the plight of all child labourers. I finished by asking, "Who wants to help?" Before I knew it, 11 hands flew up! That's when I learned that having the courage to try makes even the hardest things possible.

When the 12 of us got together that evening, Free The Children was born. None of us had much experience with social justice work. My parents always encouraged my brother Marc and me to explore our world. And they made sure we understood how important it is for people to take care of one another. But that was it. We were in new territory.

Craig Kielburger

Born: December 17, 1982

Home: Toronto, ON

Founded: Free The Children in 1995

Belief: Children have the power to change the world.

Free The Children's Seven Steps to Social Involvement

Step 1: Find your passion; choose your issue.

Step 2: Research the reality.

Step 3: Build your dream team.

Step 4: Hold a meeting.

Step 5: Set your mission; set your goals.

Step 6: Take action.

Step 7: Have fun!

A Trip of a Lifetime

In the beginning, our main goal was to raise awareness about child labour. But many of the people I was speaking to would often ask whether I'd ever met any child labourers. This got me thinking. What better way to find out how to help child labourers than to ask them? There was only one problem: I wasn't even allowed to take the subway by myself, much less travel halfway around the world. I wasn't sure how I would convince my parents.

As luck would have it, a family friend, 24-year-old Alam Rahman, was planning a trip to South Asia and generously invited me along. My parents trusted Alam, and before I knew it, the trip of a lifetime was taking shape.

I met Alam in Dhaka, Bangladesh. From there, we started a seven-week tour of Bangladesh, Nepal, India, Pakistan, and Thailand. From the moment we left the airport in a rickshaw, it was clear that we were in a different world.

One of the first places we visited was a sprawling slum just outside the city.

In the blistering heat that afternoon, I saw poverty up close. Curious children wearing dirty rags ran to us, their stomachs bulging because of poor nutrition. Homes were little more than bits of cardboard and tin. There were no buildings, schools, or hospitals.

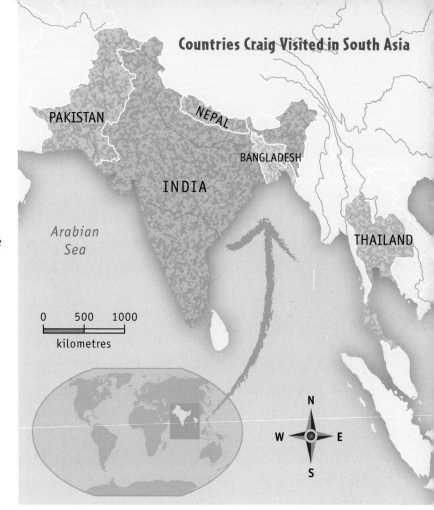

Countries Craig Visited in South Asia

"What better way to find out how to help child labourers than to ask them?"

25

I was in tears. I managed to ask a local human rights worker, "How can I help?" To my surprise, he told me to go home and describe to my friends the suffering I'd seen. He encouraged me to ask them whether it was fair that some people have so little in our world of plenty.

This advice stayed with me throughout my trip. I'd expected child labour to be a secret, but everywhere we went, children were out working in plain view. In India, I met children who'd spent their entire lives making bricks out of mud. In a factory, I spoke to an eight-year-old girl who pulled apart used syringes (needles) to sell the parts. She worked without shoes or gloves. Many times, she got pricked by the dirty needles, putting her at risk of getting AIDS. She'd never even heard of the disease.

Every day, I was sickened by the things that children had to do to survive. Again and again, I was told it was the only way people living in poverty could survive. I was amazed by the courage and capacity for kindness and fun in every child I met. In the most desperate places, we laughed and played together.

Students at one of the schools set up by Free The Children in Sierra Leone, Africa

I wanted to help each of the children I came to know. But I couldn't. Slowly, I came to realize that the one way I could really make a difference was by sharing their stories just as the human rights worker in Bangladesh had advised.

I also began to understand that we had to convince the children of the world that we weren't too young to bring about positive change.

Craig with young volunteers involved with Free The Children

When I returned to Canada, life in our Thornhill, Ontario, home changed forever. Requests for information started to pour in, with students from across the country wanting to know how they could become involved with Free The Children. Our organization began to take off and continues to grow today.

Even now, I still can't believe Free The Children has grown from a group of 12 twelve-year-olds into the world's largest network of children helping children. Our yearly campaigns now involve more than 100 000 young people. We are as determined as ever to build a better world.

MEDIA WATCH

Find news stories about children's rights. Who is involved in helping? Who are the children?

DIG DEEPER

1. Make an illustrated timeline to show the main events in Craig's work for children's rights.

2. Cut out newspaper headlines related to respect and human rights. Arrange them to create a poster or display that gives an important message.

This mural was created for the International Conference on War-Affected Children and to celebrate the Decade of the Child. By Art City Kids, Winnipeg, 2000.

Respect

How can a mural capture the idea of respect?

The title of this mural is "Let Only Good Spirits Guide You." It was created in 2004 by Chandler McLeod, a member of Hollow Water First Nation in Manitoba.

MEDIA WATCH

Find a photograph or other image that shows respect. Write a caption that explains your choice.

DIG DEEPER

1. With a group, discuss the symbols in one of the murals. How do they represent respect? Share your ideas.

2. Sketch a design for a mural that would show respect in your community. Share your design with a group.

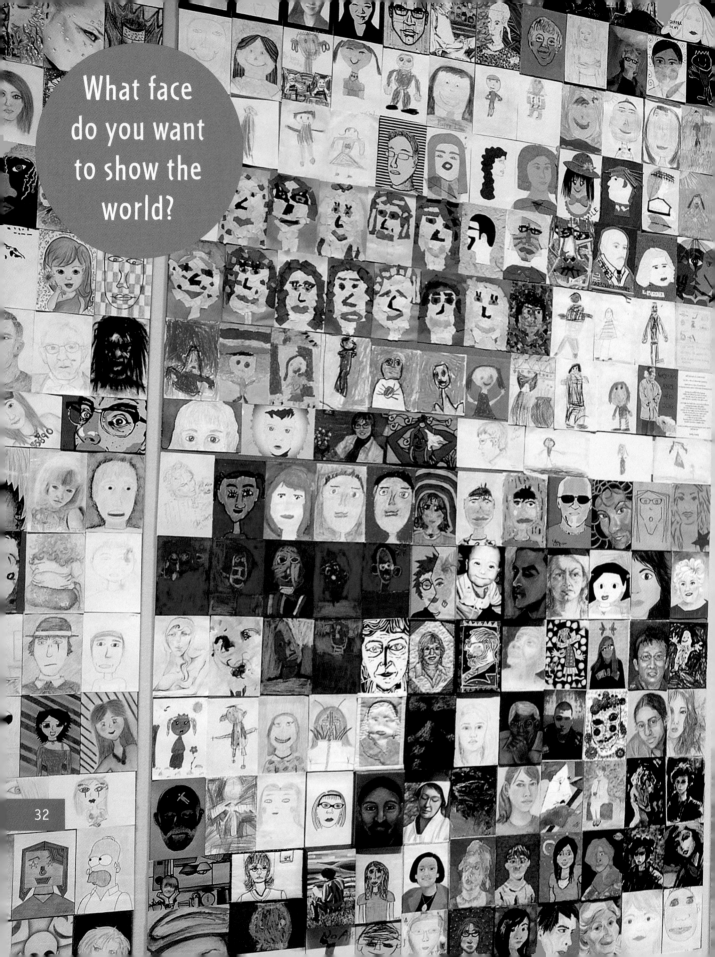

What face do you want to show the world?

32

FACES

A self-portrait is about how you see yourself and how you want others to see you. Imagine walking into an art gallery full of self-portraits sent in by people from around the world. You would see how people have expressed their individuality. Your self-portrait could join the others on the wall, too. After all, how cool is your face?

DIG DEEPER ....

1. Choose one of the self-portraits that is interesting to you. What does it tell you about the person who created it? Share your ideas with a group.
2. Create your own self-portait. Think about the face *you* want to show the world. Make a classroom gallery.

33

There Is No They,

by Monique White Butterfly

How does it feel when you are included?

They

When I feel like a
they is when they don't
talk to me.

When I feel like a they
is when they avoid me.

When I feel like a they
is when they call me
names.

When I feel like a
they is when they don't
feel sorry about what they
did.

When I feel like a they
the day feels darker.

Us

When I feel like
an us is when they
talk to me.

When I feel like
an us is when
they include me.

When there is
an us I feel happier.

When I feel like
an us the sun
shines brighter.

Only Us

DIG DEEPER

1. Work with a group to present an oral reading of the poem.
   Have some people act out the poem as you read.

2. Write a poem about how it feels to be included or about why
   it is important to include everyone. You can use the poem as a
   model or write an acrostic poem using the letters of "include."

35

Producers at Work!

Think about a TV game show you've seen or heard about. Today it is your turn to create a TV game show about respect.

Design a TV Game Show

With a group, brainstorm ideas for a TV game show about an issue related to respect. Think about:

- what you want your viewers to learn or think about
- what contestants will have to do
- who the contestants will be
- who else may be included (e.g., judges, announcers)

TIPS

- Think about how you can contribute to your group.
- Remember to be an active listener!

Prepare Your Script

- Make a set of storyboards showing the main parts of your show in order.
- Use your storyboards to create a more detailed outline of events.
- Write short biographic profiles or introductions for each of your contestants.
- Create an introduction for your announcer to read that explains the game.

Present Your Show

- Assign roles and practise your show.
- Invite others to watch and give you feedback.
- Ask them to notice how you use your voices and actions, and how well you work together.
- Videotape your show or perform it "live" in front of your audience.
- In your group, think about what went well and what you could improve. Use feedback from your audience to help you reflect on your work.

CRITERIA

- How will you know that you have done a good job?
- What do you want your audience to notice about your show?

AUDIENCE FEEDBACK

Think of two or three questions to ask your audience after the show. Have them write their answers so you can collect them.

37

The Language of Friendship

READ LIKE A WRITER

What do you notice about how the writer has divided her ideas into paragraphs?

I knew right away that Lena was not going to be your ordinary new student. My first hint? Her parents came in the week before she was to start school to speak to our class. As it turned out, I was right. Lena and her 10-year-old sister had just been adopted from Russia. Although their new mom spoke fluent Russian, Lena had not had the opportunity to learn English. Her mom asked us to help Lena adjust to her new surroundings.

My teacher asked me to be Lena's guide and study buddy. We got along right from the start. In the beginning, we had to depend on hand signals and facial expressions a lot. My new friend really can speak with just the look on her face! She is so-o-o expressive!

We did a lot of giggling in those first few weeks. At the end of our first week, I told Lena that I would see her on Monday. Looking completely innocent, she asked me why I would not be in school on Saturday—in Russia, everyone went to "Saturday School." Then she burst out giggling to show that it was just a joke. We also laughed about how funny the English language can be. One time, I said that her sweater was "cool," and she assured me that it was not cold; it was just right.

Язык
ДРУЖБЫ
by Tori Schnoor

The school counsellor gave us each a Russian-English dictionary, which we used quite a bit for a while. Because the Russian alphabet is different from the English alphabet, we often found ourselves looking up words and then just pointing to them so the other would get the meaning. Unfortunately for me, I'm not learning much Russian, because Lena is learning English way too fast!

Lena and I have been friends for eight months now, and although I think her English is outstanding (she spells better than I do!), she thinks she has a long way to go. The bond between us is so much more than just being classroom study buddies. I think it's amazing that girls born on opposite sides of the world who've grown up speaking different languages can have so much in common, and I'm so glad that fate put us together. Friendship really does have a language all its own!

How can you include someone who doesn't speak your language?

DIG DEEPER

1. Make a chart or web showing three of Lena's qualities or characteristics. Give evidence for each.

2. Choose a word or expression that shows friendship and respect, such as "Welcome" or "friend." Find the word in five languages and learn to say it.

My Gran's

Sophie's nanna bakes sponge cakes as high as my school bag and fills them with shiny strawberries and clouds of whipped cream.

But my gran's different.

Michael's grandma wears lipstick as bright as a clown's nose and leaves big smudges on his cheeks when she kisses him.

But my gran's different.

Jonty's granny catches the train to the game every week. She wears a black and white hat and screams at the referees.

But my gran's different.

Different

by Sue Lawson
and Caroline Magerl

READ LIKE A WRITER

How does the author use
repetition to emphasize
her ideas?

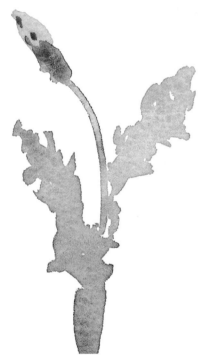

Raffie's nonna drives a florist van. She delivers roses,
daffodils, and irises all over the city.

But my gran's different.

Claire's oma used to live in Holland. She wears wooden
shoes called clogs when she works in her garden.

But my gran's different.

Alex's grandmother knits all weekend. She makes
Alex scarves as long as skipping ropes, and sweaters
that scritch and scratch his neck.

But my gran's different.

Rosie's Gramma Joan and Uncle Pat are touring the
States in an RV. They send her postcards from every
town they visit.

But my gran's different.

Mitchell's nanny owns an art gallery on Main Street and
teaches people about dot paintings.

But my gran's different.

43

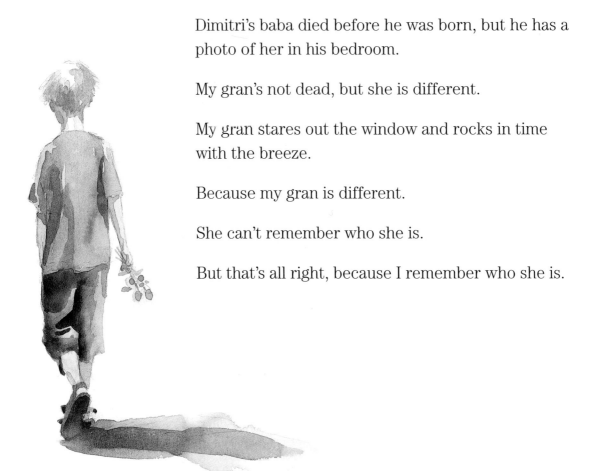

Dimitri's baba died before he was born, but he has a photo of her in his bedroom.

My gran's not dead, but she is different.

My gran stares out the window and rocks in time with the breeze.

Because my gran is different.

She can't remember who she is.

But that's all right, because I remember who she is.

DIG DEEPER

1. Make a new section for this story. Include an illustration or photograph about your own gran or another elderly friend or relative.

2. Interview an older person in your family or community to find out about his or her life. Write a biography telling about one event that was important to this person.

READ LIKE A WRITER

How does the writer connect the ending of the story to the title?

46

the FLOW

by Claire H. Blatchford
Illustrated by Janice Lee Porter

How can you tell when other people want to include you?

All the kids were staring at me. All 22 of them. I could feel their eyes going over my sneakers, my jeans, my T-shirt, my crewcut, my behind-the-ear hearing aids. It was like I was an alien that had fallen out of the sky.

My face burned. I hate it when people stare at me.

I looked at Mrs. Willcox, the Grade 5 teacher. I caught a couple of the words on her lips, "...can't hear...speak slowly..."

Then she pointed, first at me and then at the door. A woman had entered the classroom. It was my interpreter, Mrs. LaVoie. Why did she have to come on my first day? Nobody would want to talk to me with a grown-up following me around.

"Hi, Mark. How are you?" Mrs. LaVoie signed and mouthed the words silently to me across the room.

The whole class was watching us.

"This is dumb!" I signed back.

"They've never met a deaf kid before," she replied. "They..."

I didn't wait for her to finish. I had to get out of there. I raced down the centre aisle, nearly tripped over the leg of some big, long-haired guy with a smirk on his face, and ran out the door.

Mrs. LaVoie found me in the gym under one of the bleachers. She put a hand on my arm.

I pulled away. "I didn't want to come here," I told her. "My sister didn't want to come either. But we had to. Dad got a new job."

"I understand," she said.

How could she understand? She didn't know what I'd left behind—the mountains, the ski team, Jamie...

By now, Mrs. Willcox and the principal were there too. Mrs. LaVoie touched my arm again.

"I'll help you," she promised.

I didn't move. I wasn't going back to that classroom.

I saw the worry in Mom's eyes when I got off the school bus. I knew from her face that Mrs. LaVoie had called and told her I'd spent the day alone in the gym. You don't have to have ears to hear things like that.

Sarah, home early from school, was in the kitchen. Her rusty red ponytail whipped the air as she turned to face me. "I heard all about it! They say I have a freak of a brother."

"The teacher made me stand in front of the class. They were staring at me."

Sarah rolled her eyes. "You think you're the only one? They stared at me too. What do you expect when you change schools in October?"

"But I'm deaf!" I said.

"Deaf!" Sarah shook her head as she made the sign. "So deaf you won't listen to anyone—not even the interpreter they got for you?"

I went upstairs, two steps at a time. I slammed the door of my room shut, climbed over a mountain of boxes, and flopped face down on my bed.

All I could think was: *Come on, Sarah! How would you like having to sit with someone Mom's age? How would you feel if the teacher asked for volunteers to take notes and none of the kids put up their hands?*

And then I wondered, *Am I a freak?*

I fell asleep. Being deaf is tiring. You have to look, watch, listen, and figure out what's going on all day long. It was like this before too. But at least there were other deaf kids, kids that knew signs.

They were staring at me.

49

Dad's hand woke me, pressing down on my shoulder. I almost didn't open my eyes. I was sure he was mad.

"Suppertime," he said. His blue eyes seemed far away behind his thick-rimmed glasses.

I nodded.

"I heard about today," he said.

I shrugged.

"When you make a change, the first few days are always the hardest."

I didn't say anything.

"Did you hear me?" Dad asked.

The words popped out before I could stop them. "Dad, can I go back? Maybe I could live with Jamie."

Dad's eyebrows went up. They do that when he doesn't know what to say. He doesn't really know Jamie's parents. They're deaf and they only sign.

"If you did that, you'd never talk," Dad said.

"Signing *is* talking."

"I know, but..." His eyebrows rose again. "So...you're comfortable with Jamie's family?" he asked.

I paused to think about it. Jamie's parents don't think I'm really deaf. I wasn't born deaf, the way they were. I had meningitis when I was three, and everyone in my family but me can hear.

All I knew then was that I wanted to be skiing with Jamie when the snow came. I'm faster than he is, but he's sharper on the corners. Really sharp.

Dad waved to get my attention. "I tell you what, Mark," he said. "I'll think about it. But you have to promise to try one week of school here."

I put a hand over my mouth to hide my grin. *One week? That's nothing.*

Signing
is
talking.

It was cold and grey the next morning. I wondered if it was snowing where I used to live. I'd tried calling Jamie three times on my TDD—that's a telephone device for the deaf—but no one answered. Where was he? Had he forgotten about me already?

At school, the big guy I'd nearly tripped over was sitting on my desk. My stomach tightened. What was going on?

When he saw me coming, he hopped down. "I'm...eeeth," he said.

Eeeth? "Teeth?" I asked.

He nearly fell over laughing. The other kids laughed too.

Mrs. LaVoie tapped at my arm. "He's telling you his name." She spelled it out with her fingers. "K-E-I-T-H."

My face started burning again. Keith, not teeth. Some words look alike on the lips. Why had I opened my big mouth?

Keith held up a notebook and a pencil.

"I'm...taking...notes...for...you," he said.

I wanted to sink through the floor and out of sight. I hate it when people mouth everything and talk like I'm two years old. Everyone was watching us.

Only one week of this, I thought grimly as I reached for the chair to my desk.

Mrs. LaVoie's lips and signs were easy to read. At noon, she said she was going home for lunch and would be back after recess.

Keith dropped a couple of tightly folded pages on my desk and ran out.

The only free seat I could find in the cafeteria was near some Grade 3 kids. I read a book so I didn't have to look at them while I ate. I wasn't very hungry.

When I stepped outside at recess, I saw a bunch of guys playing basketball. They were really into it. Their tongues were almost hanging out of their mouths.

Only one week of this.

I wanted to watch them, but I didn't want them seeing me.
I turned to go and **whack!** Something hit me hard on the
neck. There was Keith, his long hair plastered to his sweaty
head. I knew from the way he was grinning that he'd thrown
the basketball on purpose.

"Come play," he gestured.

I glared at him. He'd called me just like you'd call a dog. I would have gone back inside except for the look on his face. I could hear it as clearly as I hear the thoughts in my own head: *What a wimp! Is he going to run away and hide again?*

I put the book and my lunch box down and walked onto the court.

"You're...on...*my*...team," Keith said, using preschool language again.

"You don't need to talk so slowly," I told him.

"Oh—" The way Keith said it, I realized he wasn't sure I could really talk.

One of the guys tossed the ball to me. I caught it and ran off dribbling.

They were fast, but I was faster.

I ran this way and that. Around them, between them, maybe even under them. Anger can give you speed.

I took a wild shot, missed the basket, dove for the ball, got it, and dropped it.

Someone tripped me up from behind. I went flying, hands first, onto the pavement.

It was Keith.

"You—*you* did that?" I yelled.

He waved his fist at me. "Who do you think you are?" he yelled back. He was talking fast now. "*I'm* the captain. You do what I tell you."

We stared at each other. I could have quit, but I didn't want to. It's weird, but I *had* to find a way to stay on that team. I *had* to show him I could do it the way he wanted.

I got up. The palms of my hands were stinging, but I didn't look at them. "What do I do?" I asked.

Keith paused and scratched his arm. "Watch," he replied.

Watch? That's what I do all the time.

"Flow," he added. "Yeah, go with the flow."

They were
fast,
but I was
faster.

54

I didn't try to call Jamie that night. I was too busy thinking about Keith and basketball. When I skied, it was my speed against Jamie's speed. This was different. I'd never really played *with* other guys on a team before. Would Keith ask me to play again?

For the next three days straight, I played basketball with Keith at recess. Sometimes I could see the others shouting and laughing. I couldn't understand them and felt really out of it. Sometimes Keith and the others shoved me around. Once when that happened, I got angry. Keith had tripped me again. I was ready to punch him. But when I saw the look on his face, I suddenly knew he wasn't trying to make me mad. He was just trying to tell me how to flow.

Friday, after the last bell, Keith dropped his notes on my desk.

"Thanks, but I don't think I need them," I said.

He frowned. "How come? Aren't they good enough for you?" he asked. He was angry. It was like I'd tripped *him*. Neither of us said anything then because Mrs. Willcox was coming toward us wondering what was going on. We didn't want her in on the conversation.

"I'm not sure I'm coming back," I told him when we were outside. "That's why I said that about the notes."

His mouth fell open. "But you just got here," he said.

I told him about Jamie and my old school.

He was just trying to tell me how to flow.

"You can't go...." Keith was talking a mile a minute now, jumbling the words, gesturing wildly. I had to make him say it over.

He told me that tryouts for the basketball team were coming up soon. "You've gotta try out," Keith said, grabbing my arm. "You're fast, you're smart, and you don't need ears like everybody else to hear what's going on.

"Besides," Keith went on, "if you made the team, we could use sign language."

My bus pulled up then. I had to go. When I looked out the window, Keith put two fingers up in a big V. I read the words on his lips, "We need you."

We need you. No one had ever said that to me before. It felt good.

Well, that was two months ago, and I'm still here. And, yes, I'm on the basketball team. I'm teaching the guys some sign language. It comes in handy when we're playing other schools!

Keith still trips me up every now and then when I get going all by myself on the court. He still takes notes for me too. (Some of his notes are really about basketball, but don't tell!)

I'm not saying everything is fine. When you're deaf, you're always deaf. You can't get over it the way you get over a broken leg or a headache. People forget to look at you when they talk. Or they forget to slow down a little or not mouth everything. Or they have trouble understanding what you're saying.

I know there will always be times when I feel left out. But that's okay. I'm learning to go with the flow.

We need

you.

58

DIG DEEPER ••

1. Choose an event in the story. Role-play Keith telling his family about Mark and what happened.

2. Make a chart showing at least three ways the students in Mark's new class showed respect and tried to include him.

Connect and Share

It's your turn to share information you've learned in a guessing game! Choose a real person from this unit or someone else you have researched.

Create a challenge!

■ Use "I" as if you were that person.

■ In role, write a list of facts about "your" life and what you did to become famous.

■ Don't tell your name!

Share with your family

■ Tell your list of facts to your family.

■ Remember to say "I" as if you were the person.

■ Ask them to guess, "Who am I?"

■ Together, make up "Who am I?" challenges about other people.

■ Share one of your family's challenges with a partner or group at school.

TIPS FOR SPEAKING IN ROLE

• Remember to say "I."

• Try to use the person's voice.

• Speak clearly so your audience can hear.

Spotlight on **Learning**

Collect

- Gather your notebooks, writing, and projects from this unit.

Talk and reflect

Work with a partner.

- Together, read the Learning Goals on page 2.
- Talk about how well you met these goals.
- Look through your work for evidence.

Select

- Choose two pieces of work that you are proud of and that show how you achieved the Learning Goals.

Tell about your choices

- Tell why you chose each piece and what it shows about your learning.

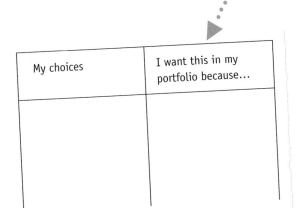

My choices	I want this in my portfolio because...

Reflect

- What have you learned about biographies and other ways of sharing events in someone's life?
- What does "respect" mean to you? Which selections or activities have had the biggest impact on your ideas about respect?

61

Hooked on Ads

LEARNING GOALS

In this unit you will

- View and analyze the messages in advertisements.

- Compare various forms of ads.

- Learn how to become "ad smart."

- Create and present advertisements.

product
messages
target audience
point of view
marketing

63

Ad Smart
by Peter

What does it mean to be "ad smart"?

Ads are everywhere!

Hi, I'm Peter. I've been digging around to learn about the tricks of the ad trade. Trust me, in this mad ad world you've got to be "ad smart."

You see an ad for a product...you buy it. Your friends see it...they buy it. The next thing you know, nearly everyone in the schoolyard is wearing the same styles, buying the same brands. No big deal?

It's big business. From government messages like no-smoking campaigns to product ads for skateboarding shoes, North American advertisers spend $2.7 billion per year promoting their messages—and trying to sell you on what's the ultimate in cool.

Add It Up

The average kid sees between 20 000 and 40 000 ads each year on TV. And when you count all the other ads you see—everywhere from fridge magnets to Web site pop-ups, bathroom stalls to bumper stickers—you are probably looking at 16 000 ads a day!

Why all the attention from advertisers? It's because you're a very important customer. Across North America, kids like you spend more than $100 billion every year on clothes, candy, games, DVDs, music, movies, and food. Plus you also have a say in close to $300 billion in purchases your parents make—for everything from computers to family vacations—and even the family car. It's no accident those car companies are featuring cartoon characters in their ads.

65

Selling Shoes— and Style

Check out this shoe ad to uncover some of the common techniques advertisers use to sell to you.

LET'S TALK ABOUT IT...

- Talk about your favourite ads or commercials, including why you like them. Decide which techniques from this article they use.

- In groups, take turns acting out your favourite commercials, changing them a bit if you like. Challenge others to decide which techniques your commercials use.

You

MaXimum **Grip**
MaXimum **Grind**
MaXimum **Cool**

Turn some heads while you do some triX

You could risk buying something else. But it's not like you to take a chance.

Rule the Halfpipe!

The power's in your hands ...er—on your feet.

And it's coming from the new **X-ultra**

Best board shoes I've tried.
- Tony Eagle

Pure shoe. Pure you. **X-ultra**

- **Flattery** will get you customers. If you make people feel good, they're more likely to buy your product.

- Make 'em laugh. **Humour** is one of the most successful ways to persuade you to buy.

- From skater shoes to cell phones, ads use **fun illustrations and animation** to appeal to kids.

- Ever notice that in most ads, skaters are cool while good students are nerdy? **Stereotypes** are an easy—and unfair—way to send messages.

- Already forget the name of these skater shoes? Don't worry. You'll remember the **logo**.

- X-ultra shoes can't really guarantee maximum grip, grind, or cool. But hey, ads often **exaggerate the facts**.

- Advertisers figure if **popular celebs** promote a product and love it, why wouldn't you?

- The **expert says** it's the best—so it's got to be, huh? Or is he on the payroll?

- Change your shoes and you'll change your life. Advertisers count on people **buying into the dream**.

- But boarders like you take chances, right? Oh yeah, **you get the joke**. And advertisers are hoping you'll buy their product to prove it.

- Ads use **slogans** like "Pure shoe. Pure you." so the message they're selling—and the product—will stick in your head.

67

Viewing Advertisements

Ads are created for a specific purpose and a specific audience. Think about an ad you have seen on TV, in a magazine, in a store, or on the Internet.

TALK ABOUT IT!

- What was the product?
- Who was the target audience?
- What caught your attention or influenced your thinking?
- What kinds of ads do you see around you every day?

Work with a partner. Talk about all the places you see ads. Make a chart together.

Advertisements

Product	Location of ad	What caught our attention
– T-shirt	– sports magazine	– favourite athlete is in the ad

Think Like a Viewer

- Why do people look at ads?

Crack the code

- When you see advertisements, be aware of how the advertiser has used such techniques as words, font size, colour, images, and sounds to influence your thinking.

Make meaning

Practise using these strategies when you view ads:

USE WHAT YOU KNOW
What does the ad remind you of?

DECIDE WHAT'S IMPORTANT
Think about the purpose of the ad. What does the advertiser want you to think or do?

EVALUATE
Ask yourself if the ad is giving accurate information.

Analyze what you see

- Ask yourself if the ad is missing a point of view. Why would this be important to know?

69

Better Than Being There!

Be a Winner!

Wired Sounds!

Be "On the Edge" with NEW and IMPROVED Wired Sounds!

Reflect on Your Viewing

You have . . .

- viewed and analyzed different forms of ads.
- learned how a team works together to create ads.
- learned new vocabulary about advertising.

product   messages

target audience

point of view   marketing

Hey, look at this... Buy one, get one free! That sounds like a great strategy!

You have also . . .

- practised strategies to become "ad smart."

USE WHAT YOU KNOW

DECIDE WHAT'S IMPORTANT

EVALUATE

Write About Learning

Write about why it is important to understand how ads work. Explain how knowing advertisers' techniques will help you when you view ads.

View Like an Advertiser

Graphic designers try to make their ads eye-catching and convincing. When they design an ad, they think about the target audience and the purpose of their ad.

TALK ABOUT IT!

- What do you notice about the images and words in ads?
- Make a list of techniques advertisers use when they create ads.

HINT!

Think about how **images** and **words** hook the viewer and create emotion.

Advertising Techniques

- use words, slogans, and font styles to attract the viewer's attention

- use colour to create mood or feeling

- use specific words to persuade the viewer

- place the information so that it catches the viewer's eye

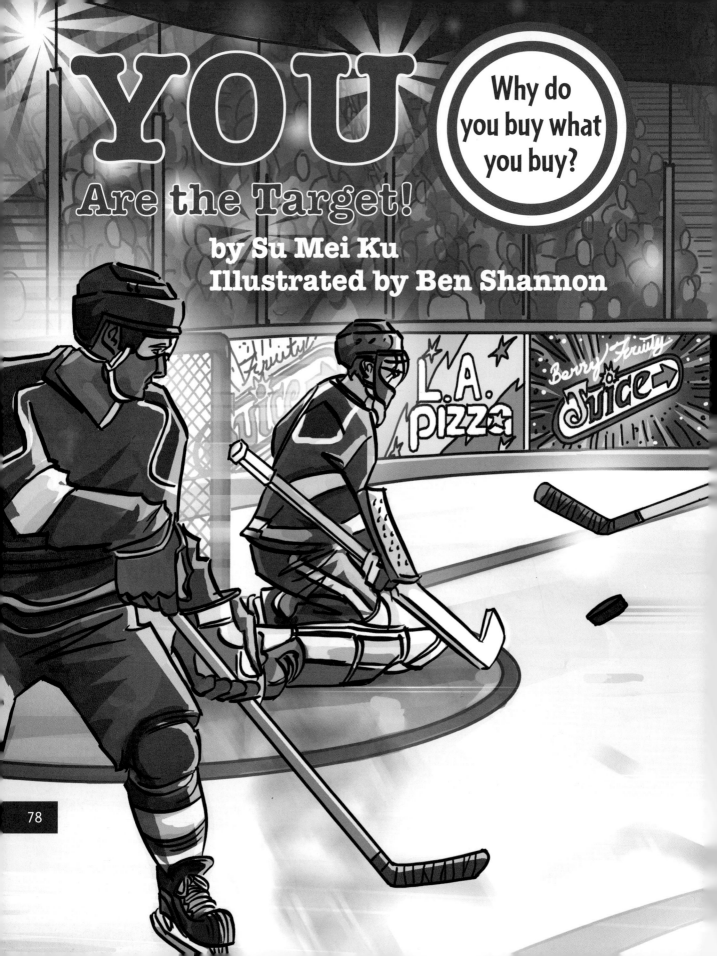

YOU

Are the Target!

Why do you buy what you buy?

by Su Mei Ku

Illustrated by Ben Shannon

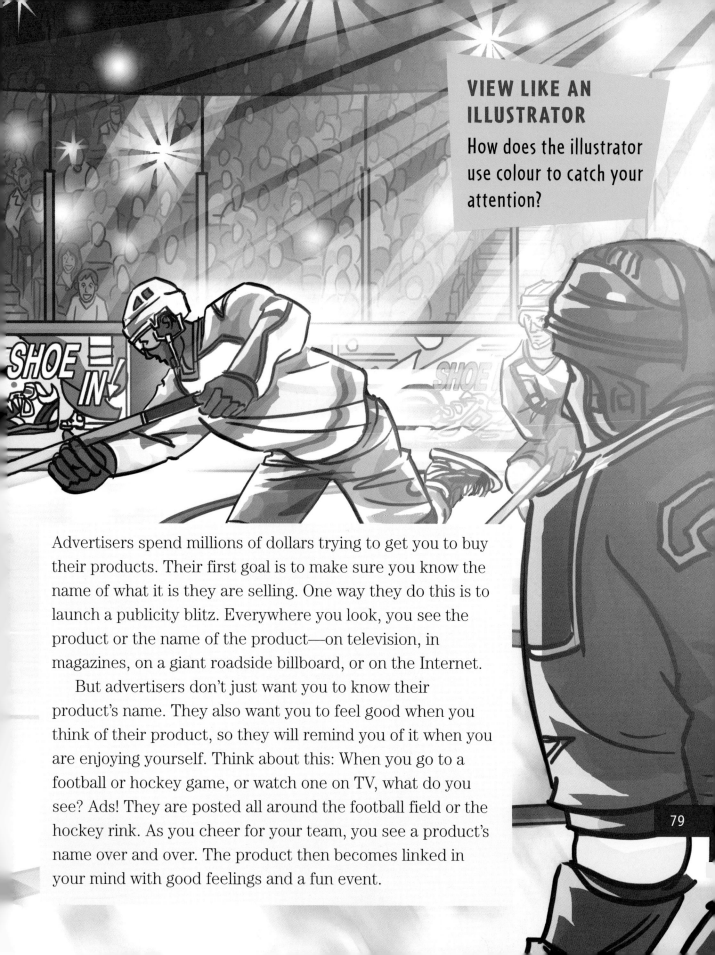

VIEW LIKE AN ILLUSTRATOR
How does the illustrator use colour to catch your attention?

Advertisers spend millions of dollars trying to get you to buy their products. Their first goal is to make sure you know the name of what it is they are selling. One way they do this is to launch a publicity blitz. Everywhere you look, you see the product or the name of the product—on television, in magazines, on a giant roadside billboard, or on the Internet.

But advertisers don't just want you to know their product's name. They also want you to feel good when you think of their product, so they will remind you of it when you are enjoying yourself. Think about this: When you go to a football or hockey game, or watch one on TV, what do you see? Ads! They are posted all around the football field or the hockey rink. As you cheer for your team, you see a product's name over and over. The product then becomes linked in your mind with good feelings and a fun event.

Look for product placement and "virtual" ads (ads that can only be seen by the television audience) when you are watching sports events on TV. Analyze which types of products you see most often.

Some athletes are paid millions of dollars each year to display their sponsor's logo.

Products also appear on TV programs and in movies. This strategy is called *product placement*. When viewers see their favourite actor using a product, they often decide to use it too. But did you know that TV and movie stars are paid a lot of money to eat a certain brand of cereal, wear clothes with a company logo, or just to say a company's name? Musicians are also paid big sums of money to use product names in their songs. Sometimes a famous person becomes a *celebrity spokesperson* for a certain product. The celebrity may be paid to appear in actual ads for the product, or just to be seen using it.

Advertisers have found that some young people can often influence their friends and classmates. With instant text messaging and blogs, word spreads like wildfire.

Some parents fear that advertisers have more influence on their kids than they have. They worry that advertisers aren't interested in helping you learn what is right and wrong, healthy and unhealthy. Advertisers just want to sell a product. What do you think?

Some advertisers use young people in their ads. They hope that other young people will imitate them by wearing or using the same products.

DIG DEEPER ••••••••••••••••••••••••••••••••

1. View the ads on pages 78–79 and identify the products. Talk about who produces these ads, who pays for them, and who benefits from them.

2. Brainstorm a list of places in your community where you might display an ad for an upcoming art show at your school. Which places do you think would be the most effective? Why?

Food Tricks

You Should Know About! by PBS Kids

How do advertisers make the food in ads look so appealing?

Foods can look perfectly delicious, thanks to the work of a food stylist. Food stylists are like make-up artists and it's their job to make the food you see in advertisements look great. However, when you discover how they achieve this perfect look, you might just lose your appetite.

82

VIEW LIKE AN ADVERTISER
How do visual images help to promote a product?

Roasted Chicken

If you don't want to get sick as a result of eating raw meat, you have to cook a chicken thoroughly—all the way through. But a fully cooked bird has ugly wrinkles when it comes out of the oven, so you must use some tricks to get picture-perfect, golden smooth skin.

RECIPE

- 1 chicken
- dishwashing soap
- 1 roll paper towels
- needle and white thread
- pins
- red and brown food colouring or molasses mixed with water, oil, and a drop of soap
- blowtorch
- stuffing

1. Wash the chicken with plenty of detergent to clean off any fat from the surface. Turn the chicken over and pull the skin tight, and sew up with a needle and thread. Pull the neck skin tight and pin. Stuff the bird well with plenty of wet paper towels. This keeps the bird plump and creates steam.

2. Tie the legs securely with thread. Roast the chicken until the skin becomes bumpy and dry, but with the inside still uncooked. Brush or spray the bird evenly with colouring mixture until it reaches the perfect brown colour but remains plump and juicy looking.

3. Need more colour? Use a blowtorch to brown the legs, wings, and any parts that may still look pale. (Don't try this at home!) Finally, spoon on a heap of stuffing to cover up the paper towels inside. Still feeling hungry?

83

Ice Cream

Advertisements to sell ice cream must use pictures of the real thing, but if the ads are to sell hot fudge or whipping cream, then the ice cream can be faked. Fake ice cream is a food stylist's best friend because it looks just like the real thing, but fortunately, it never melts.

RECIPE

- Shortening or margarine
- Powdered sugar
- Corn syrup
- Vanilla beans, strawberry jam, cocoa, or other colouring and flavourings

Mix the ingredients together until evenly combined. This fake ice cream is smooth like clay, but it crumbles just like real ice cream when scooped. Best of all, you can keep it for months in a plastic bag, and it will still look good. But do you wonder how it will taste?

DIG DEEPER ●

1. Which trick surprised you the most? Why?

2. Create or find a mouth-watering photo of your favourite food. What tricks might a food stylist use to make it look good? Write your answer in the form of a recipe, like those in the selection.

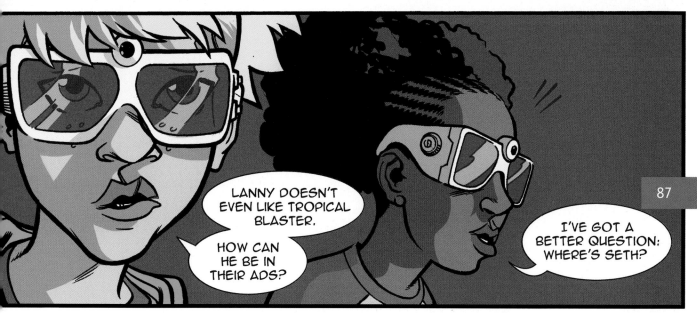

87

DOWN THE HALL...

THERE YOU ARE, SETH!

WHO ARE THESE PEOPLE?

THEY'RE THE ADVERTISING PEOPLE WHO CREATE THE TROPICAL BLASTER ADS.

TROPICAL BLASTER TASTES SO GOOD BECAUSE EACH BOTTLE CONTAINS 30 GRAMS OF SUGAR.

NO PROBLEM. WE CALL TROPICAL BLASTER A "FRUIT DRINK." WHEN PEOPLE SEE THE WORD "FRUIT," THEY THINK IT'S NUTRITIOUS!

AND HAVING A BIG SPORTS STAR LIKE LANNY CHOW IN OUR ADS ALSO MAKES PEOPLE THINK IT'S GOOD FOR THEM.

THAT'S AS MUCH SUGAR AS COLA AND OTHER POPS!

THAT MEANS WE CAN'T CALL IT FRUIT JUICE, BUT WE STILL WANT PEOPLE TO THINK IT'S A HEALTHY DRINK.

THEY'RE DISTORTING THE FACTS JUST TO MAKE THEIR DRINK SOUND HEALTHY, WHEN IT'S AS SUGARY AS COLA!

HANG ON, JANELLE.

LOOKS LIKE WE'RE ON THE MOVE AGAIN.

OOPS! GUESS I SHOULDN'T HAVE PRESSED THE "BACK" BUTTON.

DIG DEEPER

1. With a partner, discuss whose point of view is missing from this graphic story. What do you think they might have to say?

2. With a group, role-play this comic strip. Afterwards, talk about your feelings toward the ad agency and Lanny Chow.

What's Next?

by Esther Fleming • Illustrated by Christopher Hutsul

How will ads change our lives in the future?

You might think you've seen and heard it all when it comes to advertising, but you're wrong! Advertisers are always thinking of different ways to get their messages across to us. Here are some new ideas you might be hearing about soon.

Did You Say "Sleep Here" or "Sheep Here"?

A Dutch hotel paid farmers to advertise their company by dressing up sheep. For a payment equal to about $1.30 per sheep per day, farmers draped their animals in waterproof blankets with the company's logo and Web site address on them. The ad company behind the plan hopes to expand to other countries and use other livestock.

It's Raining...Ads?

A Japanese company might soon be hitting consumers with what they call "information rain." The company is developing a projector that will show images of raindrops falling on the ground. People will enter the "rainy" area and hold their palms up, as if checking for rain. The projector will then project an ad onto the would-be customers' palms.

"Hi, This Is the Coffee Shop Calling!"

Imagine your phone rings as you walk down the street. You think it might be your mom calling, or maybe your best friend. Wrong! It's an advertiser calling to suggest you drop into the store you're about to walk by. Using satellite technology, advertisers hope to send phone messages to you at the exact moment you're close to a place where their product is sold.

The Ads on the Bus Say "Buy, Buy, Buy"

Some buses in England display ads that change as the buses move. These vehicles are called "intelligent" buses. Their ads change to reflect the businesses along the bus route. Plans are being made to change advertisements based on other things too. For example, an ad for sunscreen could run when it's sunny, then change to an ad for umbrellas if it gets cloudy.

DIG DEEPER

1. Choose one of the ideas or innovations that interests or surprises you. Explain your reaction.
2. Think of an original way to use technology for advertising. Write a description of your idea and include a sketch. Share with the class.

VIEW LIKE AN ILLUSTRATOR

How does the illustrator help you understand the information?

Online Marketing Strategies

by the Media Awareness Network
Illustrated by Ben Shannon

What do you know about online marketing?

Online advertisers use many strategies to try to get kids to buy their products. Often, they blend advertising with activities and games on the Internet. Kids may not even recognize that the advertisers are trying to sell to them. Next time you're on a commercial kids' site, see if you can spot any of these strategies.

Some marketing strategies, like banner ads, are pretty obvious.

Others are more subtle. Imagine a giant commercial that kids can enter, where they can play with products and talk with product "spokescharacters." Imagine a commercial that gives marketers access to information about specific kids, including their innermost dreams and desires. This is what the Internet offers advertisers through commercial Web sites.

VIEW LIKE A MARKETER

How can visuals be used to make a sales pitch look like fun?

93

Here are some of the strategies used by advertisers to involve kids in their products:

- Virtual environments that make kids feel as if they are entering an actual place. Look for words like *world*, *village*, *town*, *clubhouse*, and *planet*. Companies want children to feel that this is not a commercial—it's a special world that's been created just for them. Some Web sites ask children to type in their names before entering a site, in order to provide them with personalized greetings when they return.

- Friendly, cartoon spokescharacters that encourage kids to identify with products and companies. Advertisers are hoping that brand recognition at a young age will evolve into lifelong brand loyalty.

- Interactive games and activities like crossword puzzles and word searches that feature brand-name products and their spokescharacters. Traditional advertisements don't work on the Internet, so advertisers seamlessly blend advertising content with games and activities.

KidsSportsPlanet

sell information about kids to other companies, and make the advertising on their Web site even more effective!

What's the bottom line? Recognize when advertisers are trying to sell to you. Commercial sites are lots of fun, but they exist to make money. When you visit commercial kids' sites, see how many online marketing strategies you can spot.

- Downloadable screensavers featuring products and spokescharacters, or e-mail "postcards" that can be sent to other kids via the Web site. (The company that owns the Web site can then add these additional addresses to its database.)

- Clubs that kids can join, and contests they can enter to win prizes. (Many of the prizes feature product logos, slogans, or characters.)

Kids are often asked to give out personal information like their names, e-mail and home addresses, phone numbers, and preferences before they can join clubs, enter contests, or play games. This enables marketers to contact kids through e-mail,

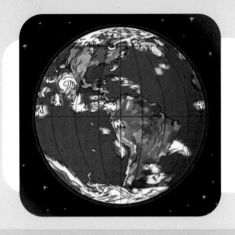

Canadian Kids in a Wired World

Kids with an Online Message

by Cara Bafile

Not all Web sites are about commercial advertising or product promotion. Students in Arviat, Nunavut, recently became historians and reporters as they interviewed local Elders about the Inuit way of life. The interviews were part of an effort to create a Web site to preserve Arviat's heritage and the Inuktitut language.

"The most rewarding part for me was interviewing the Elders," says May T., a student who contributed to the Web site. May did research, typed the stories in Inuktitut and English, and took digital pictures of the Elders.

"I'm hoping that visitors to the Web site will learn all about the different kinds of shelters that Inuit used throughout the year," May explained. "I also hope that the Inuit who visit this site read the Inuktitut pages, not just the English pages. That way they can improve their Inuktitut reading skills."

Researchers were interested in learning how Canadian kids, like you, use the Internet. Here are some facts they discovered about Grade 5 students who went online during an average school day. Many students used the Internet for more than one activity.

- About **88 out of every 100** played games.

- About **60 out of every 100** worked on a topic of personal interest.

- About **26 out of every 100** worked on their own Web site.

DIG DEEPER ·················

1. For one week, keep a record of how much time you spend on the Internet and the activities you use it for. Make a graph to show your data.

2. With a group, brainstorm a list of things kids can do to be safe and responsible online. Share your list with other groups.

Ads: They're Not ALL Bad!

by Allan Badali

How can ads help to inform us?

It would be impossible to avoid all advertising. In fact, advertising can be used to inform us and raise awareness about key issues.

Think of the good results that can come from advertising. It can teach us about our country.

Fisheries and Oceans Canada   Pêches et Océans Canada

Integrated Management   Marine Protected Areas   Marine Environmental Quality   Gestion intégrée   Zones de protection marines   Qualité du milieu marin

PLANNING • COOPERATION • EDUCATION • CONSERVATION • COMMUNITY INVOLVEMENT

PLANIFICATION • COOPÉRATION • ÉDUCATION • CONSERVATION • IMPLICATION COMMUNAUTAIRE

Our Oceans, Our Future
Nos océans, notre avenir

Canada

97

VIEW LIKE A
GRAPHIC ARTIST
In what ways are the
photos and illustrations as
important as the words?

How long should you wash your hands?
Imagine singing
Happy Birthday,
twice.

While handwashing is the single most effective way to stop the spread of infections, most people don't wash their hands thoroughly enough, long enough, or often enough. Here's how to do it right:

1 Remove your jewelry.

2 Turn on the water. Make sure it's warm.

3 Wet your hands and apply soap.

4 Rub your hands together for at least 20 seconds. Pay particular attention to your fingernails and the areas between your fingers.

5 Rinse your hands from the wrist to fingertips. Keep fingertips pointed down to prevent recontamination.

6 Dry your hands with a paper towel. Drying your hands properly is as important as washing them.

7 Use the paper towel to turn off the faucet.

Always wash your hands thoroughly:

- Before, during, and after you prepare food
- Before eating
- After using the bathroom

- After sneezing, coughing, or blowing your nose
- After touching your eyes, ears, nose, or mouth
- After touching commonly used items

For an online demonstration or more information about infectious disease, visit **WorkSafeBC.com**.

WORK SAFE B
WORKING TO MAKE A DIFFERE

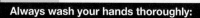

Through the hands of our Elders ...

Our stories. Our culture.

A way of life passed from
one generation to the next.

Our relationship to the
land and water, along with
healthy, active living.

Keeps our Nation strong.

It can give us
information that will
make our health better
or our work safer.

Our Health: Strengthened by Sharing

The Métis Centre is dedicated to providing a better understanding of Métis health issues. If you would like to know more, please contact us.

Métis Centre, National Aboriginal Health Organization Toll Free: 1-877-602-4445 http://www.naho.ca/metiscentre

Megamunch Club

Megamunch Club:
fall/winter 2006

A Saturday morning program,
perfect for 5-8 year olds!
9:30-11:30 a.m.

Oct. 14: "The Colours of Fall"
Exploring the change in seasons
and discover what happens when
the leaves start to fall!

Oct. 28: "Critters of the Night"
Learn all about creepy crawlies
that go bump in the night -
wear a costume for a
Halloween treat!

Nov.11: "Age of the Volcano"
Come with us while we explore
the time before Dinosaurs roamed
the Earth!

Nov. 25: "Age of the Dinosaurs"
Learn all about the age of
these ruling reptiles!

Dec. 9: "Life after the Dinosaurs"
Discover the changes that
took place after the dinosaurs
died out!

Dec.23: "Holiday Cheer"
Join us for our last Megamunch
club of 2006, with our very own
holiday celebration!

Each day includes a gallery visit,
story time, crafts, games and
a snack.

$40 for complete season
($35 for RSM members)
OR individual dates $7/child

Registration begins September 14
through the RSM gift shop
or call 7͟5͟7͟-͟5͟9͟5͟1͟ with a credit card.

RSM A:
787-81
www.r

It can inform us
about exciting
activities we might
want to get involved
in or new ways to
have fun.

Capture the 4-H Spirit!

4-H is about fun,
friendships, and tons of cool
stuff to do. November is
National 4-H Month in Canada.
Contact us to find out how
you can join the fun today . . .

NATIONAL
4-H MONTH LE MOIS
NATIONAL DES **4-H**

WWW.4-H-CANADA.CA

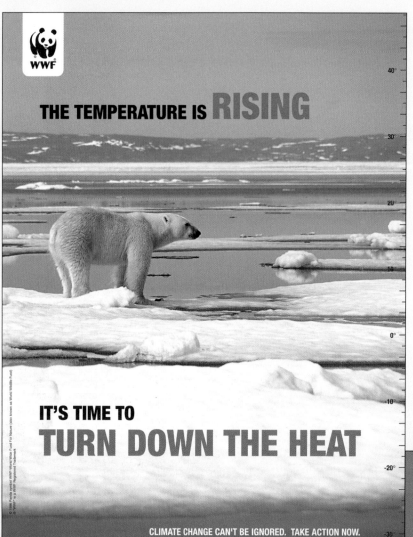

Most importantly, advertising can highlight events and causes that are important to our lives and to the wider world in which we live.

DIG DEEPER •••••••••••••••••••••••••

1. Which ad had the greatest impact on you? Write about why you connected to it.
2. Search for ads and posters that deliver positive and important messages. With a group, sort them into categories. Report on what you notice.

MEDIA WATCH

Look for public service ads in newspapers and magazines, and on walls and bulletin boards in public places.

101

Advertisers at Work!

The form of an advertisement often has an impact on its message. Choose a form that you would like to explore, then work with a partner to advertise a product.

Plan an Advertisement

Brainstorm ideas for your ad.

- Identify a product and the target audience.
- Think about the purpose and message of your ad.
- Choose a form that will best represent your product.

Plan and sketch ideas.

- Will your ad take a particular point of view?
- Will you use photos, drawings, or real people?
- What feelings do you want to create in your audience?

IDEAS TO TRY

- Design a T-shirt to raise money for a homeless shelter.
- Create an ad that shows that a product's packaging is important.
- Present a pet food commercial.

Design the Ad

- Write the words or script.
- Create the images.
- Choose the layout or camera angles.

Revise and Rethink

- Do all these techniques work together to clearly present your message?
- Will your ad influence the consumer?

Present the Ad

- Present your ads to each other. Use expression to show that you believe in what you say.

Reflect

- How effective were the messages?
- Why were some forms of advertisements more powerful than others?

Sidewalk Circus

by Paul Fleischman and Kevin Hawkes

104

105

DIG DEEPER

1. Think of another funny pairing of a sign with a real-life event. Draw a picture of the scene, including the sign.

2. Why might two people "see" the same picture or event differently?

109

The Kid from the Commercial

Adapted by Aaron Shepard
from the book **It's New! It's Improved!
It's Terrible!** by Stephen Manes

What might happen if your favourite TV
commercial character came for a visit?

ACTORS

Narrator 1   Narrator 2   Arnold   Will   Mr. Schlemp

Will:	(*with a wide smile, and speaking in a TV announcer's voice*) Hey! Don't change that channel!
Narrator 1:	Arnold was almost afraid to look, but he forced himself to turn around. All the slime that had poured out of the broken TV set was gone. It had magically changed into a boy!
Narrator 2:	The boy was Arnold's age. He was tall and blond, and had bright blue eyes and a big smile. He was wearing a Helicopter Jones T-shirt and Helicopter Jones jeans and— of course—Helicopter Shoes.

READ LIKE A WRITER

A scriptwriter often puts words in parentheses right after the speaker's name. How does this help the reader?

Will:	*(spins around once and dances)*
	*Heli*copter,
	*Heli*copter,
	*Heli*copter Shoes.
	We're talk-ing
	*Heli*copter,
	*Heli*copter,
	*Heli*copter Shoes.
	(spins around again and flashes a smile)
Arnold:	You're from the commercial!
Will:	*(smiles wider)* Not just *one* commercial! Not just *two* commercials! Not merely *three*! Hey, I'm in *twenty different commercials*, each one more wonderful than the next! Isn't that *amazing*?
Narrator 1:	Arnold was too flabbergasted to say anything.
Will:	*(holds out his hand)* You're my special friend.
Narrator 2:	Arnold suddenly remembered—this kid had said those exact same words in last year's commercials for those ugly prune-faced dolls.
Arnold:	*(distrustfully)* I don't even *know* you. How'd you *get* here? Where'd you *come* from?
Will:	*(does tap step and spins around)* I come from here, I come from there, But I can come From *any*where! *(in a low voice)* Costumes sold separately.
Narrator 2:	Arnold recognized that too. It was the commercial for Mr. Mysterio, the amazing spy action-figure.
Arnold:	Who *are* you?!
Will:	*(bows, still smiling)* Will Flack, at your service. Now, just tell me one thing. What exactly are we selling?

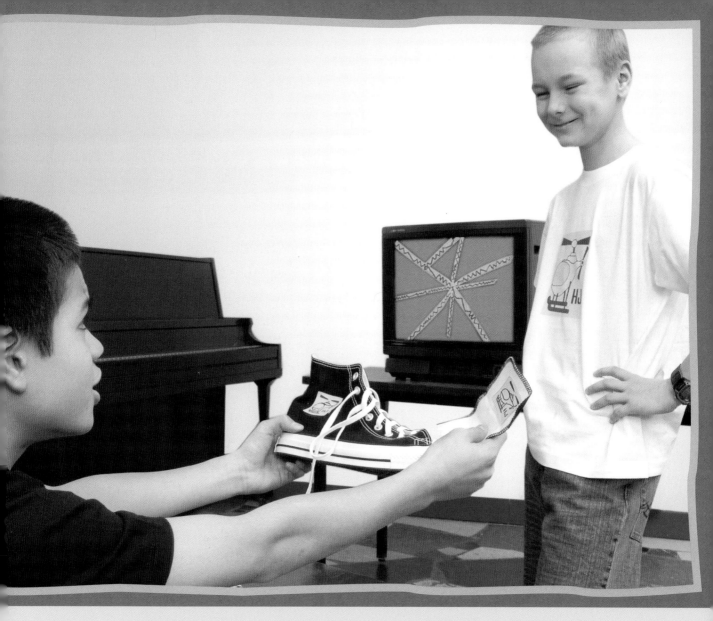

Arnold:	*Selling?* I'm not selling *anything.* Unless maybe you're interested in a broken pair of Helicopter Shoes!
Will:	Broken? What?
Narrator 1:	Arnold picked up his tongueless Helicopter Shoe and handed it to Will.
Arnold:	Broken. Messed-up. Ruined.
Will:	*(brightens)* Of course! This is our never-before-offered *detachable-tongue* model! It's new! It's improved! It's—
Arnold:	Terrible!
Will:	Terrible?
Arnold:	Terrible.

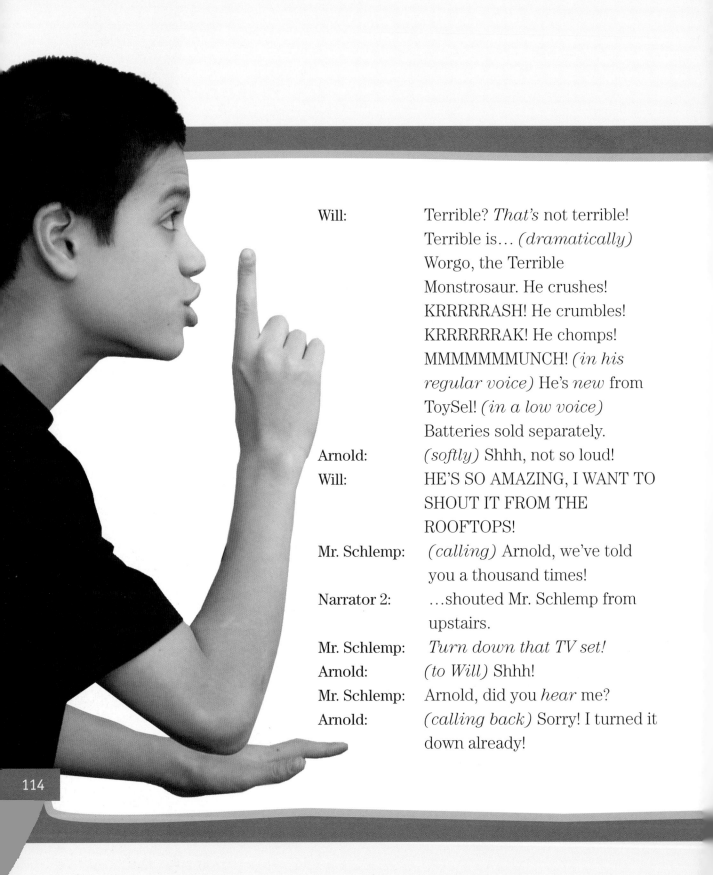

Will:	Terrible? *That's* not terrible! Terrible is… *(dramatically)* Worgo, the Terrible Monstrosaur. He crushes! KRRRRRASH! He crumbles! KRRRRRRAK! He chomps! MMMMMMMUNCH! *(in his regular voice)* He's *new* from ToySel! *(in a low voice)* Batteries sold separately.
Arnold:	*(softly)* Shhh, not so loud!
Will:	HE'S SO AMAZING, I WANT TO SHOUT IT FROM THE ROOFTOPS!
Mr. Schlemp:	*(calling)* Arnold, we've told you a thousand times!
Narrator 2:	…shouted Mr. Schlemp from upstairs.
Mr. Schlemp:	*Turn down that TV set!*
Arnold:	*(to Will)* Shhh!
Mr. Schlemp:	Arnold, did you *hear* me?
Arnold:	*(calling back)* Sorry! I turned it down already!

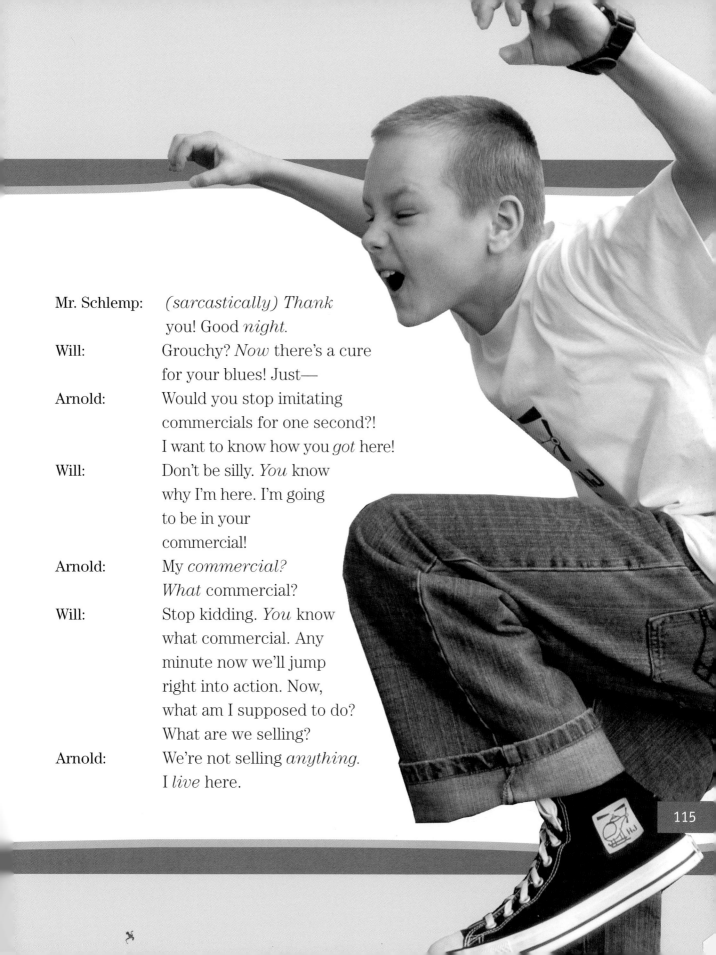

Mr. Schlemp:	*(sarcastically) Thank* you! Good *night.*
Will:	Grouchy? *Now* there's a cure for your blues! Just—
Arnold:	Would you stop imitating commercials for one second?! I want to know how you *got* here!
Will:	Don't be silly. *You* know why I'm here. I'm going to be in your commercial!
Arnold:	My *commercial? What* commercial?
Will:	Stop kidding. *You* know what commercial. Any minute now we'll jump right into action. Now, what am I supposed to do? What are we selling?
Arnold:	We're not selling *anything.* I *live* here.

Will:	*Sure* you do. At least while this *commercial's* on. *(looks around)* I know! *TV* sets! That *broken* one over there will magically turn brand-new!
Arnold:	I wish.
Will:	No problem! All I need is the script. Or I can just make something up. Let's see… "It's magic! Make your *old* TV set just like *new* with…" What are we selling, again?
Arnold:	I *told* you. We're not selling *anything*.
Will:	Right! A *public service* announcement! "Lend a hand! Donate your used TV to the charity of your choice! Just phone the number on your screen."
Arnold:	There *is* no number. There *is* no screen.
Will:	You can't fool *me*. I eat Brain Berries, the cereal that gives you the smarts!
Arnold:	*(exasperated)* I keep *telling* you. This isn't a commercial! My TV just broke! And somehow you came through it from the inside!
Will:	*(still smiling, but suddenly worried) Wait* a minute. Your T-shirt! It doesn't *say* anything on it.
Arnold:	So what?
Will:	It has to *say* something. Or at least have some little character on the front. It *has* to. It's a sacred rule!
Arnold:	Maybe in *commercials*. But I keep telling you, this isn't a commercial! This is *real life*.
Will:	"Real life"? I don't know what you're *talking* about. But whatever it is, it's easy to fix. You need… Now, just let me think. You need…
Arnold:	I'll *tell* you what I need! I need fast, *fast*, FAST RELIEF. But somehow—
Narrator 1:	Arnold looked again at the shattered TV, then back at the weird kid who had come out of it.
Arnold:	I don't think I'm going to get it.

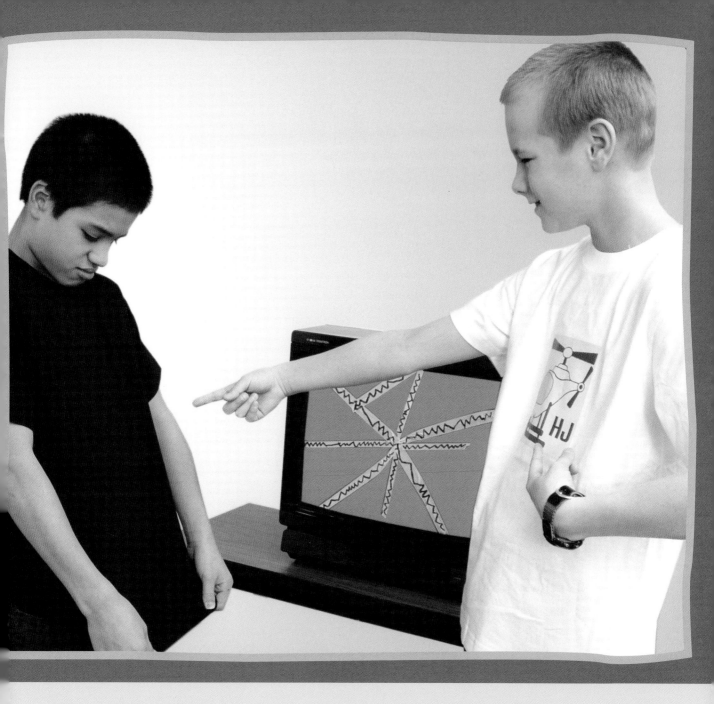

DIG DEEPER ··

1. What do you notice about the way a script is written? How is
   it different from the way a story is written? Make a chart to
   identify the characteristics of a script.

2. Practise this script as a Readers' Theatre. Present it to other
   classes in your school.

Connect and Share

You have learned that becoming "ad smart" is extremely important. Share this learning by designing a bulletin board.

Create a class bulletin board!

- Locate the best place in the school to display your learning.

- Choose an advertising piece to post on the bulletin board.

- Write captions or design a poster to share the ad smart tips you learned. Display the tips on the bulletin board.

Share at home!

- Treat your family to a "live performance" of what you have learned about advertising. Be convincing!

- Ask family members to share stories about how advertising has influenced them.

PLANNING TIPS

- Create an eye-catching title for your bulletin board.

- Plan a powerful layout— try different ways of arranging your ads and tips.

- Think about adding a border.

118

Spotlight on **Learning**

Collect

■ Gather all your advertising pieces. Include any of your brainstorming and planning work also.

Talk and reflect

Work with a partner or small group.

■ Together, read the Learning Goals on page 62.

■ Talk about how well you met these goals.

■ Look through your work for evidence.

Select

■ Choose two pieces of work that show how you achieved the Learning Goals. (The same piece of work can show more than one goal.)

Tell about your choices

■ Tell what each piece shows about your learning.

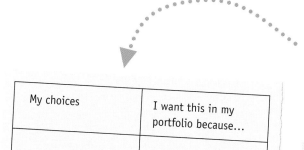

My choices	I want this in my portfolio because...

Reflect

■ What have you learned about viewing and creating your own ads?

■ What have you discovered about ads?

119

UNIT 3

Body Works

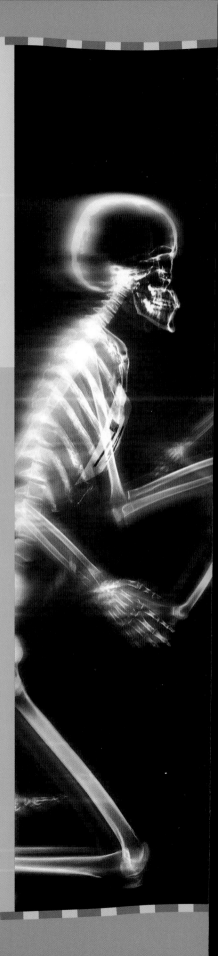

LEARNING GOALS

In this unit you will

- Read, listen to, and view selections about human body systems and healthy living.

- Compare information and share ideas about how to keep body systems healthy.

- Use scientific terms to describe different body systems.

- Research and represent information using diagrams and graphs.

120

organ systems
digestion
respiration
circulation
nutrition
exercise

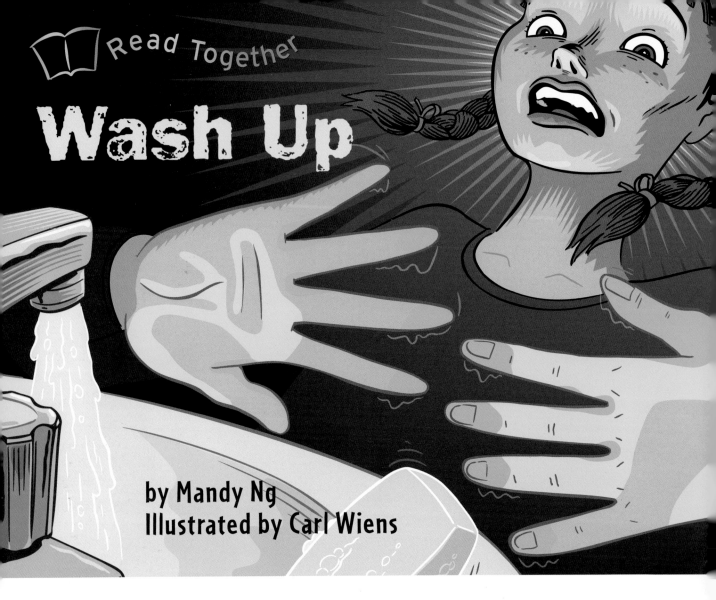

Wash Up

by Mandy Ng
Illustrated by Carl Wiens

The light green areas are often missed.

The dark green areas are almost always missed.

How can washing hands help to keep your body healthy?

Your hands come in contact with millions of germs every day. That's why experts say scrubbing your hands for at least 10 seconds is the simplest, most effective thing you can do to keep germs from spreading. Make sure to wash the most frequently missed areas on your hands, such as between your fingers and around your thumbs.

Ten Things You Might Not Know About Germs

1. Believe it or not, germs have been around for over 3.5 billion years—that's even before dinosaurs! In fact, scientists believe that for a long time, bacteria were the only life form on Earth.

2. Six out of every 10 forms of living matter on Earth are made up of germs. Bacteria, viruses, fungi, and protozoa live in the air and water, on food and plants, and even inside your body. But only 50 of all the billions of germs on Earth are harmful to humans.

Germs are too tiny to see with the naked eye. This bacterium (a single bacteria) has been magnified 73000 times.

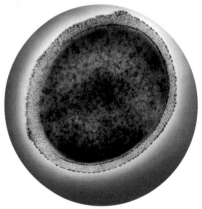

3. Over 500 species of germs live in your guts and billions of them go to work every day to help you digest your breakfast, lunch, and dinner.

4. Eating onions isn't the only way you can get bad breath. Blame it on the millions of germs that hang out inside your mouth! The bacteria secrete wastes, which can build up and cause less-than-fresh breath.

5. Surfaces where there's lots of human traffic are hot spots for germs. Certain viruses can live on a doorknob for a couple of seconds to a couple of days! Look out for drinking fountains, toilets, faucets, and desks.

6. When you sneeze or cough, droplets from your mucus—the slimy stuff inside your nose—float in the air. Breathing in these droplets is one way cold germs can spread from one person to another.

7. When germs attack, they feed on the nutrients inside your body and release toxins. That's why you feel zapped of energy when you get sick and show symptoms like fever and sniffles.

8. Get out that hanky! A single sneeze can spread over two million germs. Using a tissue or cloth when you sneeze captures 80 to 90 of every 100 active germs that you release into the air.

9. Handwashing isn't the only way to fight germs. A person who catches a lot of zzz's has a better chance of battling infections. While you sleep, your body releases chemicals that are important for your immune system—your body's defence against sickness—to stay in tip-top shape.

10. Not all germs will make you sick! Without bacteria or fungi, you couldn't turn milk into into cheese or yogourt. Also, certain foods contain "good" kinds of germs called probiotics, which some people eat to keep healthy.

Meet the Germs

Find out how these germs make us sick.

Bacteria are germs we can find everywhere. These little guys are best known for giving us strep throat, ear infections, and pneumonia.

Viruses are micro-organisms that attach themselves to our healthy cells to make us sick. Common viral infections are flu and chicken pox.

Fungi (FUN-guy) are microbes that thrive in warm, dark, and damp places like the insides of your shoes. Fungi are the main cause of athlete's foot.

Protozoa (pro-toh-ZOH-uh) are germs that live in moist places, like water. Most people who get sick from these germs get a bad case of diarrhea or bellyaches.

LET'S TALK ABOUT IT...

- What were some surprising facts that you learned about germs? Share your ideas in a small group.
- With a small group, plan a rap or a TV commercial to inform people of the importance of handwashing. Present your rap or commercial to the class.

Reading in Science

Reading and viewing can help you learn scientific facts and information. Think about a book, article, or TV program that gave you facts and information about the human body.

TALK ABOUT IT!

- Tell a partner something you learned from reading or viewing this information.

- Talk about the different places where you can find information about healthy body systems.

Here are some clues.

Make a chart showing different sources of information about healthy body systems, and give some examples.

Information on Healthy Bodies	
Source of information	Topic
– magazine article "Yoga for Beginners"	– how to do yoga safely

Think Like a Reader

digestion

Read with a purpose

- Why do you read about body systems?

Crack the code

When you see technical and difficult words about body systems, look for parts of the word you already know.

Make meaning

Practise using these strategies when you are reading in science:

ASK QUESTIONS — Look at the visuals and headings. Think about what you already know about the topic. Ask questions about what you would like to know.

PAUSE AND CHECK — Pause at the end of each section to check your understanding.

SUMMARIZE — Organize the important information in a chart or web. Include causes and effects.

Analyze what you read

- Why are "true" facts and information important in science writing?
- Why might different people explain the same science topic in different ways?

127

Your Heart

What Does It Look Like?

Your heart is about the size of an adult's fist. As you can see
from the illustration, your heart doesn't look much like those
on valentine cards! It's also not where most people think it is.
Your heart is not on the left side of your chest but in the
centre, and it has four sections. They are the left atrium
(AY-tree-um), the right atrium, the left ventricle (VEN-tre-cul),
and the right ventricle.

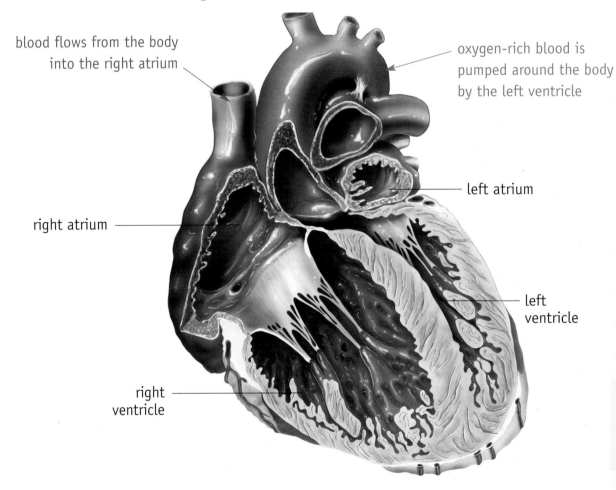

blood flows from the body
into the right atrium

oxygen-rich blood is
pumped around the body
by the left ventricle

left atrium

right atrium

left
ventricle

right
ventricle

How Does It Work?

Your heart is a muscle operated by two pumps. One pump is made up of the right atrium and the right ventricle, and the other of the left atrium and the left ventricle.

The pump on the right side sends your blood to and from your lungs to get fresh oxygen that you have just breathed in. When the blood returns from the lungs, it goes into the left-hand pump. The left side pumps this blood all around the body. The oxygen passes from the blood into billions of cells. Waste gas from these cells goes into the blood. The blood carries this waste gas back to the right side of the heart. Then the process begins all over again.

PAUSE AND CHECK

Pause at the end of each paragraph to check your understanding. Use the diagram.

Did You Know...?

Your heart, which is part of your body's circulatory system, beats about 40 million times a year. If you live to be 70, your heart will beat over 2.5 billion times!

Keeping It Healthy

The heart begins working before you are born and continues without stopping all your life. An unhealthy heart can't pump blood efficiently. This means that parts of your body might not get enough oxygen and other good things that the blood carries. Keep your heart healthy by getting lots of exercise and eating low-fat foods. Eating fatty foods can block the passages that take blood to and from your heart, and keep the blood from flowing.

SUMMARIZE

Organize the important information in a chart or web.

When you exercise, your heart pumps faster and harder because all parts of your body need more of the food and oxygen in your blood.

Your Lungs

What Do They Look Like?

ASK QUESTIONS

What would you like to know about your lungs?

Lungs are like large sponges inside your chest, protected by your ribs. Your windpipe connects your lungs to the outside air. As it goes down into your chest area, the windpipe divides and keeps dividing and branching, finally ending in little air bubbles in the lungs called alveoli (al-vee-OH-lee). Alveoli look like small bunches of grapes and are so small that you have over 300 million in each lung!

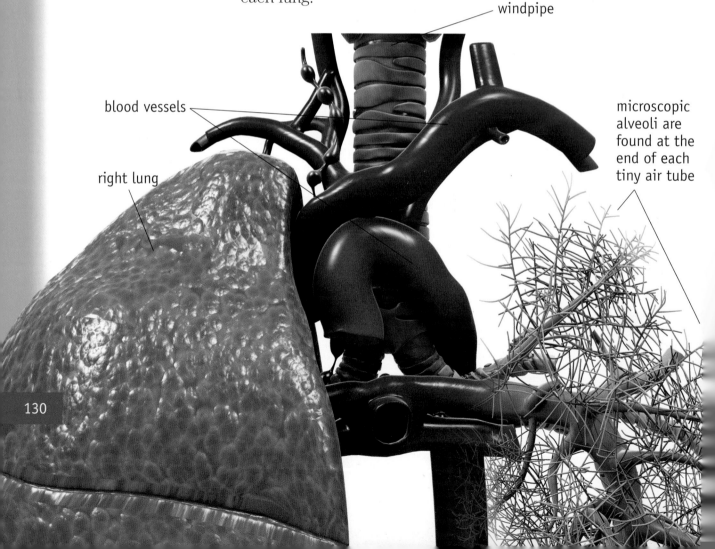

windpipe

blood vessels

right lung

microscopic alveoli are found at the end of each tiny air tube

How Do They Work?

If you put your hands on your chest, you can feel it moving in and out as you breathe. When you inhale (breathe in), your lungs become bigger and draw in air. When you exhale (breathe out), your lungs go back to their normal size as the air is forced out.

The main purpose of the lungs is to exchange air that is low in oxygen for air that is high in oxygen. When you breathe in fresh air, it goes all through the lungs and into the alveoli. Those millions of alveoli have very thin walls, so the air goes through the walls and into the blood. The blood then carries oxygen all around the body. When the blood comes back to the lungs, it contains waste gas that passes through the alveoli back into the lungs. You then breathe the waste gas out.

Keeping Them Healthy

Have you ever heard a "smoker's cough"? This is the lungs' attempt to clear out harmful substances. It is wise to stay away from areas where there is tobacco smoke. But smoking isn't the only problem for lungs. Today, if you live in a city, you might have several "smog days" in summer. Take care on those days and avoid exercising outdoors. On clear days, get lots of exercise. It's good for your lungs!

PAUSE AND CHECK

Pause at the end of each paragraph to check your understanding. Use the diagram.

Smog days are especially dangerous for seniors, children, and people with heart or lung diseases.

SUMMARIZE

Organize the important information in a chart or web.

Your Skin

What Does It Look Like?

Your skin is a thin layer that covers your whole body. It has a mass of over 3.5 kg, and if you could take it off, it would cover an area about half the size of a twin bed. Skin colour depends on the amount of a substance called melanin (MEL-uh-nin). Your hair and nails are part of your skin. About five million small, fine hairs grow all over your skin.

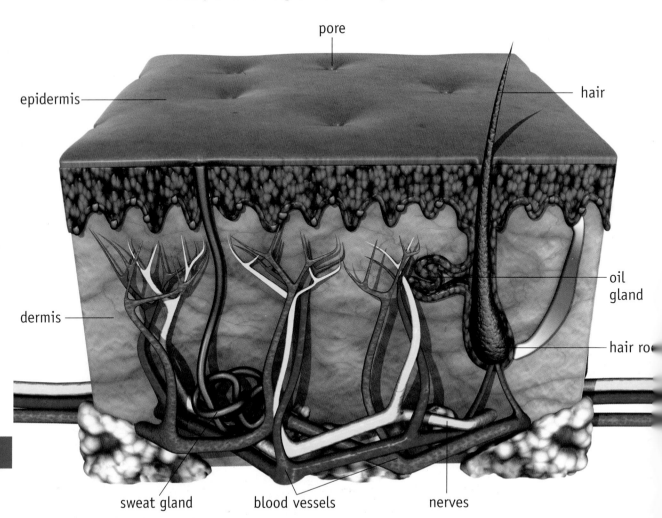

pore

epidermis

hair

oil gland

dermis

hair ro

sweat gland

blood vessels

nerves

How Does It Work?

Your skin is your contact *with*, and your protection *from*, the outside world. It helps to keep germs, water, and the sun's rays out, and it keeps your body's temperature just right. It has an outer layer called the epidermis (e-pi-DUR-miss) and an inner layer called the dermis (DUR-miss).

The epidermis has so much contact with the world, it has to replace itself continually. Every day, about 50 million dead cells drop off your skin. The dermis produces new cells and pushes them toward the surface, but by the time they reach the surface they are dead. The dermis is made up of tough, elastic fibres that connect your skin to muscles. The dermis also contains blood vessels; nerve endings that give you your sense of touch; sweat and oil glands; and the roots of the little hairs that cover your body.

Keeping It Healthy

For healthy skin, you need to eat well, exercise often, and keep your skin clean. You also need to protect your skin. The sun can damage your skin and the tissue underneath it, so use sunscreen and wear a hat, sunglasses, and other protective clothing on days when the UV index is high. (The UV index tells you how long you can be out in the sun before your skin burns.)

Did You Know...?

Your skin is part of your body's nervous system. You have a muscle at the base of every hair in your skin. When you feel cold, the muscle shortens. This pulls the hair up straight and pulls a little of the skin with it. As a result, you get goose bumps!

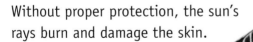

Without proper protection, the sun's rays burn and damage the skin.

133

Reflect on Your Reading

You have . . .

- talked about different body organs and systems.
- read and viewed information about how the organs of the body work.
- learned new vocabulary and scientific terms that tell about body organs and systems.

organ systems bacteria

respiration viruses

circulation

pores immunity

You have also . . .

- explored different reading strategies.

I think it's important to learn about how to keep our body systems healthy. What do you think?

ASK QUESTIONS
PAUSE AND CHECK
SUMMARIZE

Write About Learning

How did including cause and effect relationships in your summary help you to better understand the information? How can summarizing these relationships help you to read other information?

Read Like a Writer

When you were reading "Body Organs," you were reading *explanations*. The ideas in an explanation help readers understand what something is like or how it works.

TALK ABOUT IT!

- How does the writer of "Body Organs" make the ideas interesting?
- What does the writer do to help you understand causes and effects?
- Make a list of features of effective ideas in an explanation.

HINT!

Specific details will help to make the **ideas** in your explanations clear.

Ideas in an Explanation
- make clear what the topic is
- make sure all the information is about the topic
- use details to make the information easy to understand
- include information about causes and effects

135

Let's Get Moving!

by Jane Bingham

How does your body work to get you moving?

Inside your body there are hundreds of muscles and bones that work together to keep you moving. Your bones provide a strong frame for all of your body parts. Your muscles pull on your bones to make this frame move.

Bones

Together, the more than 200 bones in your body make up your skeleton. Your skeleton gives your body its shape, keeps you upright, and protects your internal organs. For example, your brain is covered by your skull, and your heart and lungs are protected inside your ribs. Your skeleton, however, is much more than just a rigid frame. All of the bones in your body are linked by joints, and most of these joints are movable, allowing your bones to move in many directions.

READ LIKE A WRITER

How does the writer help to make the explanations clear?

Inside Your Bones

This is what your thighbone looks like inside.

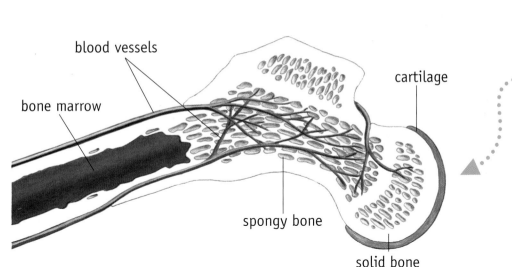

blood vessels

bone marrow

cartilage

spongy bone

solid bone

Your bones have a hard outer layer of solid bone and a slightly softer inner layer that is called spongy bone. In the centre is a space filled with jellylike bone marrow. Your bone marrow makes new blood cells. Bones need blood to supply them with food and oxygen. Blood vessels deliver blood to the spongy bone. A substance called cartilage covers the end of the bone that connects to the hip joint.

137

The Parts of the Human Skeleton

This diagram shows the main bones in your body. Every bone has a scientific name, and some have common names as well. For example, the sternum is usually known as the breastbone.

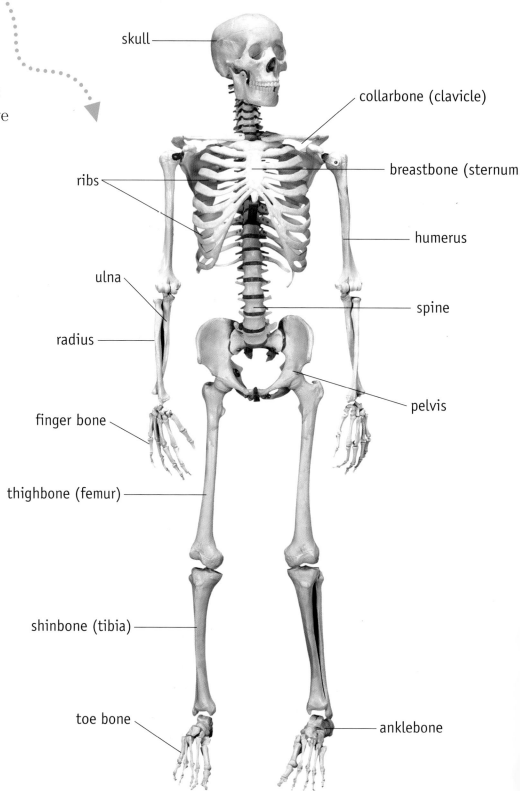

skull

collarbone (clavicle)

breastbone (sternum

ribs

humerus

ulna

radius

spine

finger bone

pelvis

thighbone (femur)

shinbone (tibia)

toe bone

anklebone

Muscles Help You Move

Muscles are responsible for every movement you make—from blinking and breathing to jumping and swallowing. Many of your muscles are attached to bones, and pull on your bones to make your joints move. But not all muscles work with bones. There are muscles in the walls of your heart that push blood around your body, and muscles in your intestines that squeeze food through your digestive system. These muscle movements happen automatically inside your body and cannot be seen at all from the outside.

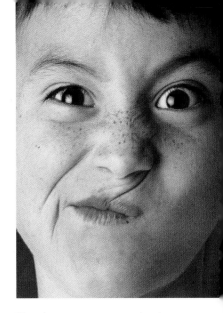

You have over 40 muscles in your face, which means you can make many different facial expressions.

How Do Muscles Work?

Muscles can make two movements: they can contract and they can relax. Muscles sometimes work in pairs, so one muscle contracts while the other relaxes. With muscle pairs that are attached to bones, one muscle in the pair pulls the bone one way, and the other muscle pulls the bone back again.

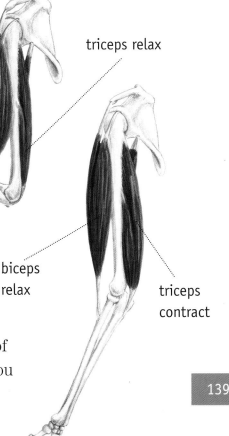

biceps contract

triceps relax

biceps relax

triceps contract

This diagram shows how the muscles in your upper arm work together. There is a pair of muscles at work. When you raise your fist to your shoulder, the muscles in the front of your arm, called the biceps, contract. They get shorter and fatter, pulling your arm up. At the same time, the muscles in the back of your arm, called the triceps, relax and lengthen. When you bring your hand back down, the triceps contract to pull your arm straight and your biceps relax.

139

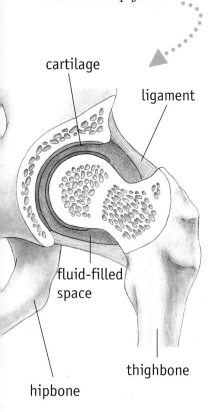

This diagram shows a hip joint.

cartilage

ligament

fluid-filled space

hipbone

thighbone

Joints

In order to move around, you need muscles, bones, and joints. It would be useless trying to move your bones if they did not have joints that allowed them to bend. There are several different kinds of joints in your body. For example, your elbow and knee are hinge joints. They work like hinges on a door that let your lower arm and leg swing backwards and forwards.

In a movable joint, the ends of the bones are covered by a flexible substance called cartilage. Cartilage is smooth and slippery and lets the bones glide over each other. The two bones are held together by tough, stretchy straps called ligaments. Inside the space formed by the ligaments is some fluid that helps the bones glide over each other smoothly. The diagram here shows a hip joint.

Growing Taller

Near the ends of each growing bone are bands made of cartilage. The cells in these bands multiply to grow new cartilage, gradually making the bone longer. By the time you are about 18 years old, your cartilage cells stop multiplying and you stop growing.

DIG DEEPER

1. Imagine you are writing to the author of this selection. What three questions about bones, muscles, or joints would you like to ask her?

2. Choose a simple activity, such as riding a bike or jumping rope, and draw a diagram to explain how the different body parts work together to perform the activity.

Your Eyes, Your Voice, Even Your Smell
Your New ID

by Rick Book

How can our bodies identify us?

READ LIKE A WRITER
How does the writer help us to understand technical words?

Every time you log on to your e-mail or favourite online game, you likely have to prove it's you with a unique password. In fact, many times a day, people use different types of ID to prove who they are. But passports, driver's licences, and ID cards can be lost, stolen, or illegally copied. People can forget passwords and PINs (personal identification numbers), and others can misuse them.

biometrics
security technology that identifies you by measuring physical or behavioural traits such as your fingerprints or your voice

But your mom was right—there's no one in the world quite like you. That's why new security technology called **biometrics** uses *what* you are to prove *who* you are. Everything from your one-of-a-kind eyes to the shape of your hand can be used to check your identity. And biometrics is almost foolproof. Our bodies are becoming our new ID cards, and we never leave home without them.

Your Body, Your ID

Here's how biometrics uses different body parts to prove who you are and weed out the fakes.

The Sweet Sound of Your Voice

Imagine there was a way to keep your little brother, sister, or friend from messing around with your computer. Nice idea, right? Well, voiceprint systems could be the trick. To set up your high security ID, you equip your computer with a microphone and voiceprint software. The computer stores a sample of your voiceprint in its memory. The next time you log on, you just speak into the microphone. The voiceprint software instantly compares this voice sample with the original voiceprint stored in its memory to see whether it's really you. If it's you, you're in!

A voiceprint is as unique as a fingerprint.

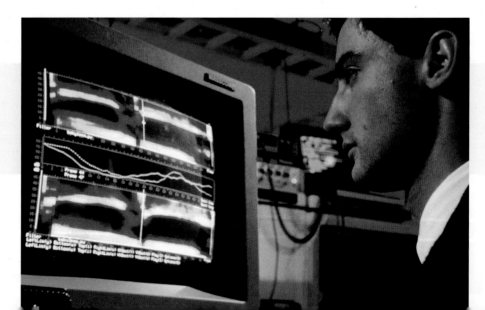

Face-to-Face

Face it—your face is one-of-a-kind. With facial-recognition technology, a computer takes a picture of your face. Then it makes a "faceprint" of your facial geometry—the distances between your eyes, cheekbones, nose, and lips. This faceprint can be compared to thousands of others on file.

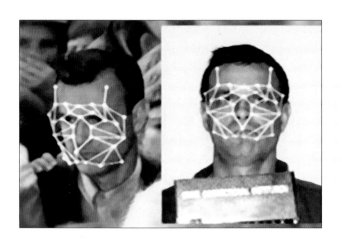

Some countries have used facial recognition in elections to stop voters from voting twice.

The Eyes Have It

The iris is the coloured ring around your black pupil. No two irises are alike, even in identical twins. Iris scanning can pinpoint over 100 unique characteristics that can be used to identify people—rings, freckles, furrows, lines, and pits.

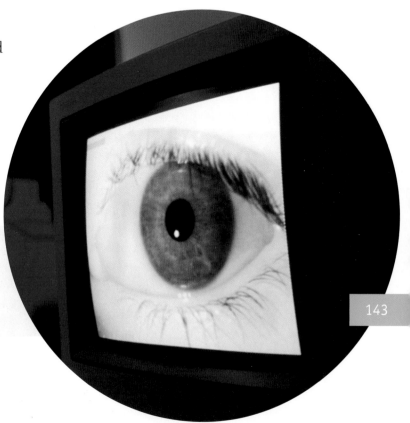

Iris scans are used by frequent flyers to avoid long lineups at major Canadian airports.

The Nose That Knows

No matter how often you take a bath, you can't cover up your own unique smell. The trick is to create an odour-sensing instrument, or "electronic nose," that isn't fooled by perfumes, diet, medicines, or even disease.

Scientists are working on a device that identifies people by "sniffing" their hands. It could be used to protect embassies and military bases.

Don't Touch That!

Police forces around the world still rely on fingerprints more than any other biometric tool to catch criminals. And now, advanced fingerprint scanners not only measure the pattern of your fingers' ridges, loops, and arches. They can also measure the height of the ridges.

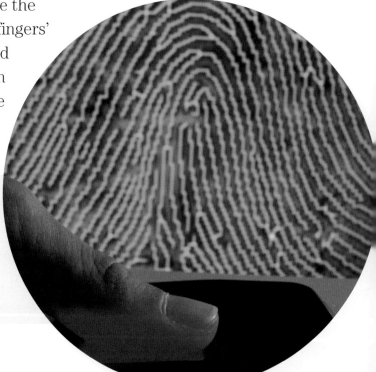

Some theme parks scan the fingerprints of visitors to make sure they don't give their entrance passes to someone else.

What Big Hands You Have

It turns out that even our hand size and shape are unique. Hand geometry scans measure the combination of the length, width, thickness, and curvature of your hand.

Some universities use hand scanning so that only students who have paid can eat at their dining halls.

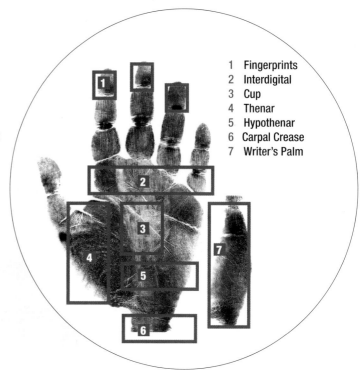

1 Fingerprints
2 Interdigital
3 Cup
4 Thenar
5 Hypothenar
6 Carpal Crease
7 Writer's Palm

Walk the Walk

The way you move could soon be enough to identify you at a glance. Gait recognition is about how we walk. Scientists are working on mapping the length and size of our legs and joints, and how they move and rotate as we strut, stroll, and sashay.

Security and police forces could use gait recognition to pick out people as they move through crowded streets or busy airports.

DIG DEEPER

1. Choose one of the ID technologies you have read about. In your own words, explain to a small group how it works.

2. With a partner, discuss the pros and cons of these new ID technologies. Make a chart to show your thoughts and ideas.

ID Technologies

Pros	Cons

145

How to Eat Like a Cat

READ LIKE A WRITER

How do the details make the information easy to remember?

Mary Catherine

Wendy

Jimmy

Mr. Bluni

Nat

Esteban

What can we learn about eating habits from cats?

by Nick D'Alto • Illustrated by Diane Dawson Hearn

Setting: Grade 5 Science class

Jimmy: Thanks a lot, Mary Catherine. You picked the hardest question for our project on cat biology.

Mary Catherine: Don't annoy me, Jimmy. I have terrible hay fever today. My nose is all stuffed up. *(Sneezes)*

Nat: What's our question?

Esteban: Here it is: "Dogs go crazy for sweet treats. But cats don't seem to have a sweet tooth at all. Research the science that explains why. Then prepare an experiment that will let everyone in class experience what it's like to eat like a cat."

Wendy: I'm stumped. Maybe cats are just finicky.

Jimmy: Maybe Mary Catherine should be finicky when it comes to picking questions.

Mary Catherine: Cheer up. At least I made us all a snack. Have some apple slices.

Jimmy: *(Bites into a slice)* Is this a joke? Yuck! These are slices of onion!

Mary Catherine: Don't be silly! *(Eating one)* They taste fine to me.

Esteban: You can't taste the onion, Mary Catherine, because your nose is stuffed up.

Mary Catherine: What?

Nat: Taste and smell work together. Like when you have a cold, sometimes you can't taste your food.

147

Esteban: And if you can't taste something, you won't want to eat it.

Wendy: Wait a minute. That's it! That's why cats don't like sweets.

Jimmy: They can't smell them?

Wendy: No—they can't taste them!

Nat: *(Reading)* You're right. In fact, this is breaking science news. In his book *So You Think You Know About Cats?*, Dr. Ronald Rosen describes how scientists have just discovered that a cat won't come for sugary snacks, because cats can't taste the flavour that we humans call sweet.

Wendy: *(At the computer)* I found the actual study. It's on the Web.

Jimmy: Keep reading. Mr. Bluni will want all the details.

Wendy:	Write this down. A **gene** is supposed to make a protein that lets taste buds detect sweetness. Then they send a signal to the brain. But in cats, that protein is missing. So cats can't taste sweet things.
Jimmy:	That's amazing. But don't cats miss eating sweet snacks?
Nat:	*(Reading another Web site)* No. It says here that cats can't even digest sugar.
Jimmy:	Wait. We eat sugary things all the time. Why would a cat's digestion be so different from our own?
Esteban:	Remember what Mr. Bluni taught us about cats? Cats are carnivores. They have an all-meat diet. And meat is just fat and protein.
Wendy:	So cats lost the ability to digest the sugars found in plants. Tasting sweet things wouldn't be important to them.
Nat:	*(Reading a book on cat health)* It says here that knowing cats have no sweet tooth is helping veterinarians develop better cat foods.
Wendy:	*(Checking a medical journal)* In fact, it's even helping doctors better understand sugar-related problems in humans, like diabetes.
Jimmy:	This is great. Now we know the science. But how can we devise an experiment that lets people eat like cats?
Wendy:	I am not eating cat food. No way.
Nat:	That's too easy. Let's just use Mary Catherine's nose.
Jimmy:	What?
Nat:	Cats can't taste sweetness because of a gene. Mary Catherine can't taste sweetness because her nose is stuffed up from hay fever. The reasons are different. But the effect is the same.

gene
A tiny part of a cell. Genes carry information that gives a plant or animal its characteristics.

Wendy:	And while we can't change our classmates' genes for sweetness...
Esteban:	...We *can* ask them to hold their noses!
Jimmy:	That's right! If you hold your nose, you can't taste as well...
Wendy:	...And that would let a human experience how a cat doesn't taste sweet things.
Mary Catherine:	Let's call our experiment "Sugar-Free Tabby: How to Eat Like a Cat."

The Next Day

Mr. Bluni:	Great experiment, kids! How did you think of it? But don't let your good grade get your noses up in the air.
Mary Catherine:	*(Still sneezing from hay fever)* Don't worry, Mr. Bluni. We're not the kind to get all stuffy about good grades.

Try the Experiment Yourself

What You Need

3 thin slices of apple
3 thin slices of onion
a partner

What You Do

1. To play the cat, just close your eyes. Then hold your nose tightly closed and open your mouth.
2. Have your partner place one slice (either apple or onion) on your tongue, without telling you which one it is.
3. Close your mouth and try to decide if it is the sweet apple or the spicy onion. (Don't bite into it or move it around in your mouth, or you will be able to tell from its texture.) Without your sense of smell, it might be difficult to tell which is which!

Try the experiment three times. How many times did you guess correctly?

DIG DEEPER

1. Imagine you are a science researcher. Write a journal or blog entry telling why your research is important.
2. Prepare a Readers' Theatre presentation of the play using simple props, voice projection, and expression. Perform for another Science class so that they can learn about this topic.

Researchers at Work!

Scientists research topics that interest them. They share their findings in a variety of ways.

An article is one way to explain your learning to others. Readers can enjoy learning about an interesting new topic.

Choose a Body System to Research

- Think about the body systems that you have read, viewed, or talked about.
- What questions do you have about body systems?
- Brainstorm ideas with a partner or in a group.

RESEARCH TIPS

- Ask your school librarian to suggest some research materials.
- Look for information in books, in magazines, on CD-ROMs, and on Web sites.
- Interview someone in the health care field about what he or she does.

Plan Your Research

- Choose a research question.
- List different resources you can use to help you find answers.
- Decide how to record your ideas and information.

Write an Article

Write an article to share your research.

Here are some important things to think about:

- Why are you writing this article and who will be reading it?
- How will you organize your explanation?
- What headings and visuals will you use?
- What details will you include?
- How will you organize your article so that it captures interest?

Display the Article

- Think of ways to share your article.
- You could collect the articles in a book and display them in the library resource centre, or create a bulletin board display.
- You might organize a Question and Answer session with another Science class about your research topic.

PRESENTATION POINTERS

- Use colour to create an eye-catching presentation.
- Use a variety of text and visual features.

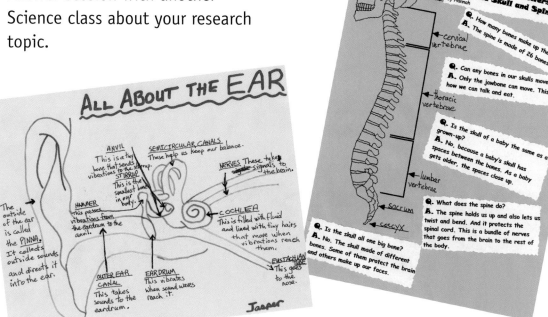

Body Verse

by Jon Scieszka • Illustrated by Lane Smith

How can poems help us to imagine the body in different ways?

Good Night

Good night, sleep tight,
Don't let the bedbug,
  tick, or louse
  suck blood from you,
  hatch its eggs,
  and then develop the larvae on you
    . . . all right?

154

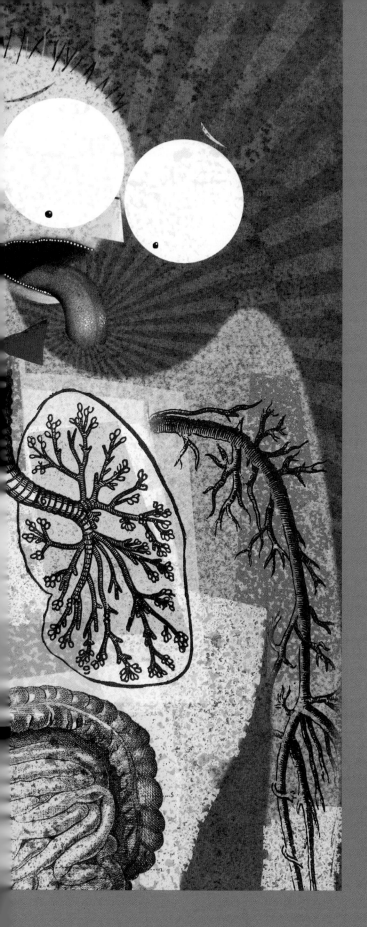

READ LIKE A WRITER
What details does the poet
use to create humour?

Lovely

I think that I ain't never seen
A poem ugly as a spleen.

A poem that could make you shiver,
Like 3.5 . . . pounds of liver.

A poem to make you lose your lunch,
Tie your intestines in a bunch.

A poem all grey, wet, and swollen,
Like a stomach or a colon.

Something like your kidney, lung,
Pancreas, bladder, even tongue.

Why you turning green, good buddy?
It's just human body study.

155

Mary Had a . . .

Mary had a little worm.
She thought it was a chigger.
But everything that Mary ate,
Only made it bigger.

It came with her to school one day,
And gave the kids a fright,
Especially when the teacher said,
"Now that's a parasite."

DIG DEEPER

1. With a group, choose one of the poems and perform a choral reading of it. Use expression and voice projection.

2. With a partner, write another funny poem about a body organ or system. Draw a funny illustration to go with it. Make a class book of your poems called *Our Weird and Wonderful Bodies*.

Hidden Worlds Magnified

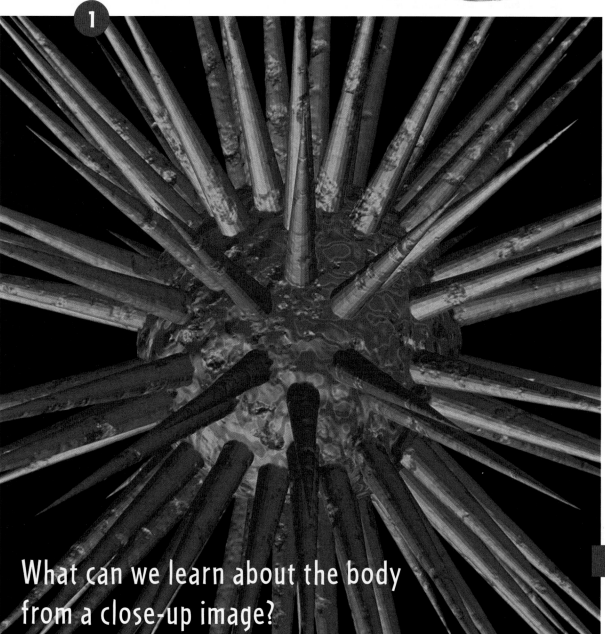

1

What can we learn about the body from a close-up image?

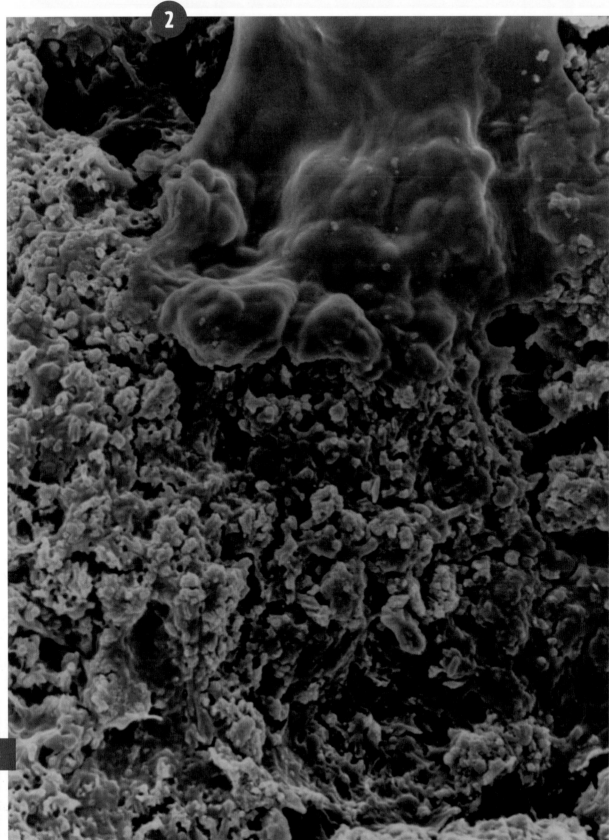

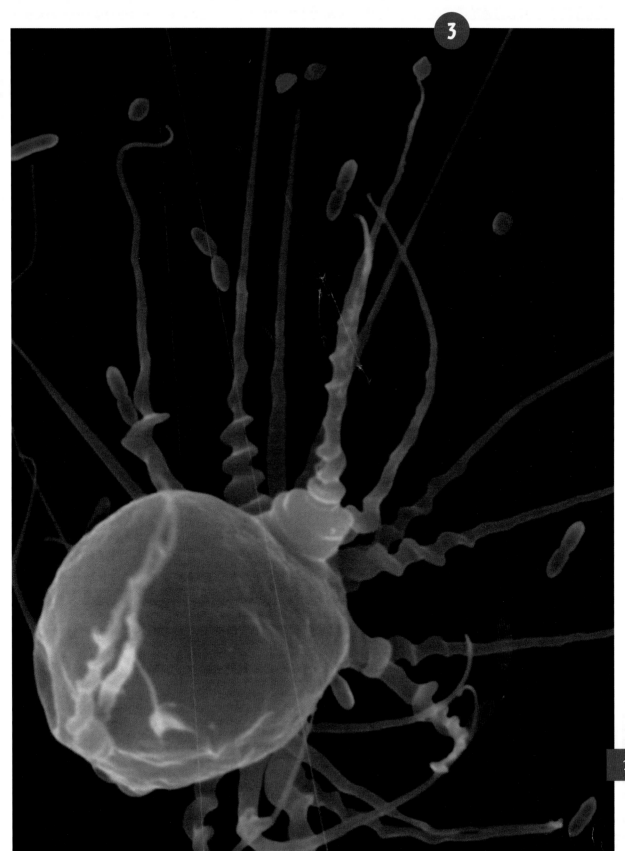

1 This "exploding star" is really a picture of a spiked virus as seen through a powerful microscope. Viruses can cause many kinds of infections, including colds and flu.

2 This image shows a tooth, magnified over 2500 times. The orange substance is plaque, and the green substance is tartar. Brushing helps slow down or prevent these substances from forming.

3 This image shows a white blood cell attacking a kind of bacteria called *E. coli*, shown in green.

4 This is a picture of healthy human skin, magnified about 500 times. Flakes of dead skin are being shed from the epidermis, the outside layer of the skin.

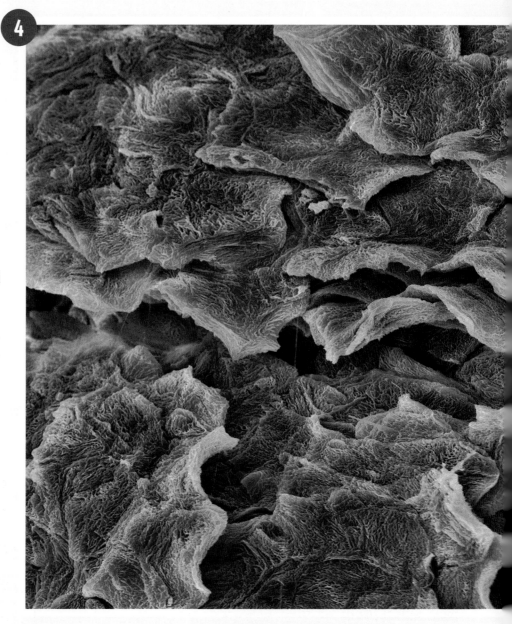

DIG DEEPER

1. Choose one of the images and write a journal response telling what it made you think about and how it made you feel.

2. Select a topic suggested by one of the images. Research some interesting facts about this topic to share with a group. Find a new image to go with these facts.

By the Numbers

Fun Facts About Our Bodies

by Rachel Proud

How fascinating can the human body be?

If all the blood vessels in the body were laid end to end, they would have a length of about 96 000 km. That means they could stretch around the world nearly 2½ times.

Your heart beats about 100 000 times every day. It pumps over 40 000 L of blood daily—that's enough to fill about 200 bathtubs.

READ LIKE A WRITER
Why might the writer use words like "about" and "nearly" so often?

An adult's digestive system is about 9 m in length. That's about as long as 2 mid-sized cars parked bumper to bumper.

When you eat a meal, you send the food on a trip that will probably last from 20 to 30 hours.

Our noses can smell at least $10\,000$ different odours. But that's nothing compared to a dog's nose. Some scientists think a dog's sense of smell may be at least 1000 times stronger than ours!

There are over SIX million air sacs, or alveoli, in our lungs. If we could open them all out and lay them flat, they would cover a tennis court.

The average person sweats about $\frac{1}{3}$ of a litre each day. On a hot day, though, we can lose over 2 L. That's why it's important to drink lots of water on hot days.

Our eyes are so sensitive that, on a clear night, it is possible to see a burning candle up to 80 km away!

DIG DEEPER

1. Find an unusual fact about the human body and draw a cartoon illustration to explain it. Make a class display of the illustrations.

2. Research some interesting facts about a particular body organ or system. Then, working in pairs, take turns being the "expert" who gets interviewed about his or her knowledge.

How Do You Rate Your Health?

by Daniel Girard

READ LIKE A WRITER

How does the author help you to understand survey information?

He's not yet a teenager, but George Abu Saleh is old enough to know he must pay more attention to his health.

A fan of junk food and television, George, 12, is trying to break bad habits. With the help of his mom, the temptation of chips, pop, and chocolate has been replaced by more nutritious choices at home and in school lunches. He also does a few minutes on an exercise machine each morning and night.

"I used to be not very healthy, but I think I'm getting better," says George.

"In my lunch, instead of chips, there's a salad," he says, triumphantly holding up a plastic grocery bag.

A survey of students like George across Toronto found the students generally know all the keys to being healthier, like eating nutritious foods and exercising more. But they don't always do a good job of following that advice.

On a scale of 1 to 5, how healthy do you think you are (1 being not very healthy or active, 5 being quite healthy and active)?

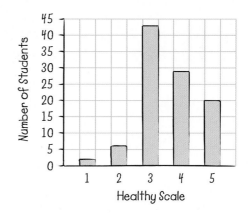

Being Healthy

How many hours on average do you spend each week participating in physical activities?

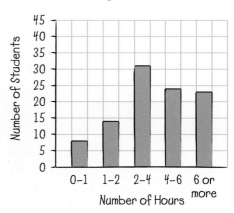

Participating in Physical Activities

165

pedometer
(pe-DOM-e-ter)
an instrument that measures the distance travelled by counting the number of steps taken

"The high number of hours they're spending on the computer or watching TV… or what they're eating shouldn't surprise us," says Lorie Shekter-Wolfson, who helped run the survey.

"But I was really surprised that, at such an early age, they are identifying they are not really as healthy as they should be."

As part of this survey, 500 students were outfitted with **pedometers** as they went around to a series of displays about such things as blood pressure and heart rates, as well as fitness activities.

Pedometer

College students (in blue T-shirts) introduced their visitors to ideas for healthy living and careers in health sciences at this display.

166

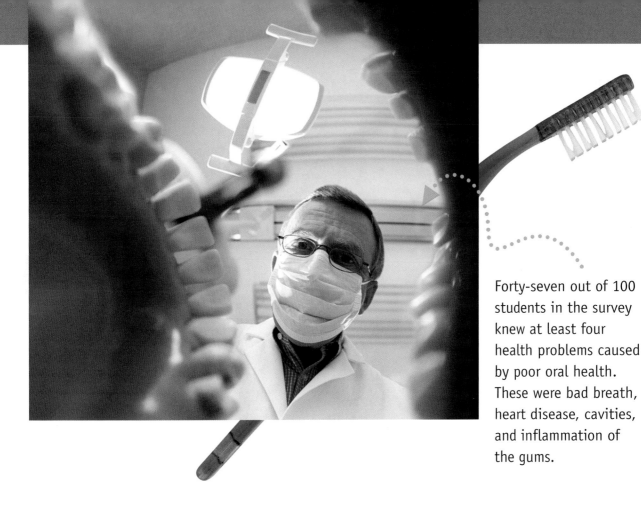

Forty-seven out of 100 students in the survey knew at least four health problems caused by poor oral health. These were bad breath, heart disease, cavities, and inflammation of the gums.

Another student in the survey, Ryan Nurse, said he and his buddies from school like video games. But they also play sports such as baseball in summer, and swim and play hockey in winter. Still, Ryan is quick to agree with his mom that getting vegetables into his diet is a problem.

"I like junk food, but I'm not eating it all night long," he says. "I know I need to eat more vegetables…"

MEDIA WATCH

Look in the newspaper for other stories about children's health and fitness. Whose ideas are given the most importance?

DIG DEEPER

1. Make a web or chart to summarize the key ideas in the health survey of students. Try to include cause and effect words.

2. Design a poster to encourage people to think about making healthy choices and promoting healthy body systems.

The Buffalo Bull
and the Cedar Tree

by Joseph Bruchac
Illustrated by Martin Gagnon

How can the Earth help to keep our bodies healthy?

When the Osage (O-sāj) people came down from the sky, they wandered the world seeking guidance and help. They wanted to learn the right ways to live and they trusted the beings they met to guide them.

The first being they met was the great Bull Buffalo. It lowered its head and bellowed with anger. It pawed the earth, throwing up red dust. Then a man of the Peace Clan fired an arrow. That arrow was fletched with Eagle's down feathers, feathers stained red with pokeberry juice to make them a symbol of peace and the dawn. The arrow entered the open mouth of the Buffalo Bull and that great one grew quiet from the magic of peace.

"I will be a great symbol for you, Little Ones," the Bull Buffalo said. Then it rolled on the ground four times. Each time it rolled, thunder rolled overhead. Then, where it had rolled, healing plants grew. The green gourd and the yellow striped gourd, the poppy mallow and the blazing star grew up from the earth where the buffalo rolled.

"I give these plants for you to use," the Buffalo Bull said to the people. "Use them and you will see old age as you travel the path of life."

READ LIKE A WRITER
Find a part of the story where the author creates strong word pictures. How does he make you see and feel what is happening?

blazing star

poppy mallow

yellow striped gourd

green gourd

169

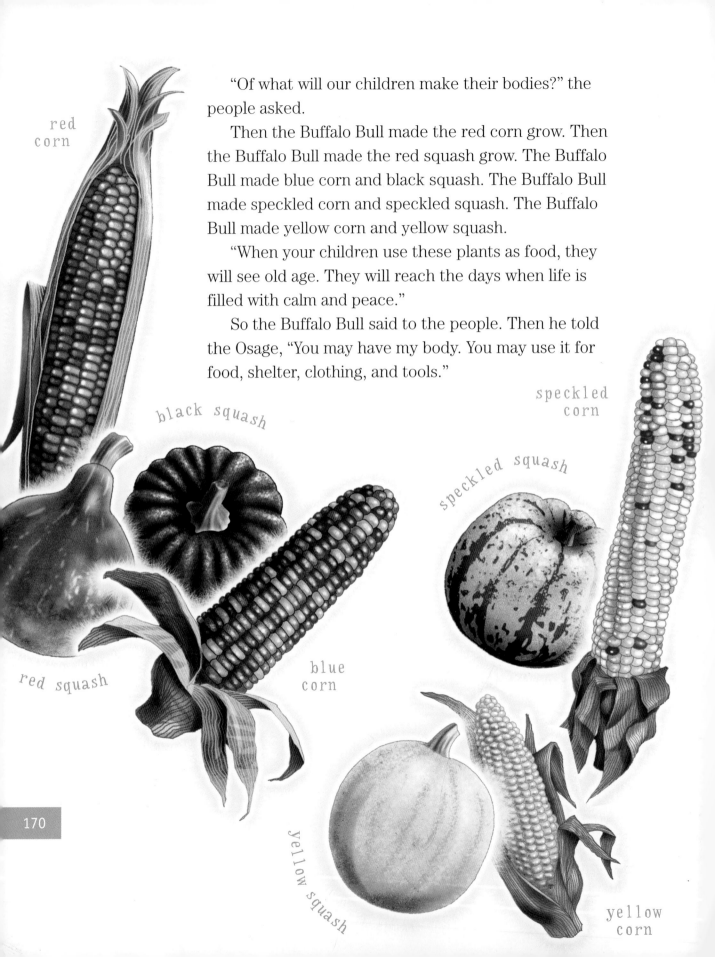

red corn

"Of what will our children make their bodies?" the people asked.

Then the Buffalo Bull made the red corn grow. Then the Buffalo Bull made the red squash grow. The Buffalo Bull made blue corn and black squash. The Buffalo Bull made speckled corn and speckled squash. The Buffalo Bull made yellow corn and yellow squash.

"When your children use these plants as food, they will see old age. They will reach the days when life is filled with calm and peace."

So the Buffalo Bull said to the people. Then he told the Osage, "You may have my body. You may use it for food, shelter, clothing, and tools."

speckled corn

black squash

speckled squash

red squash

blue corn

170

yellow squash

yellow corn

As the people continued to travel on, they saw the leaves falling from the trees. They had come to the Earth in the time of autumn. They continued to travel and the days grew colder and now all of the trees were bare of leaves. But then they came to the edge of a cliff and there before them they saw a tree whose boughs were still green. Its scent was fragrant. It was Cedar. They looked at that tree and, as she stood in the midst of the four winds, sending forth her fragrance whichever way the wind blew, she spoke to them.

"I stand here on this cliff," Cedar said, "so that the Little Ones may make of me their medicine. Look at my roots, a sign of my old age. When the Little Ones make me their symbol they, too, will live to see their toes gnarled with age. Look at my branches, how they bend. With these as symbols, the People will live to see their own shoulders bent with age. Look at the feathery tips of my branches. When the Little Ones make these their symbols, they will live to see their own hair white with age as they travel the Path of Life."

So it was that the Osage people accepted the cedar tree as their symbol of the Tree of Life.

DIG DEEPER

1. Draw an illustration for an important scene in this legend.
2. The Osage people were guided to make choices to bring them a long life. Make a list of ideas to guide people today towards a long, healthy life.

171

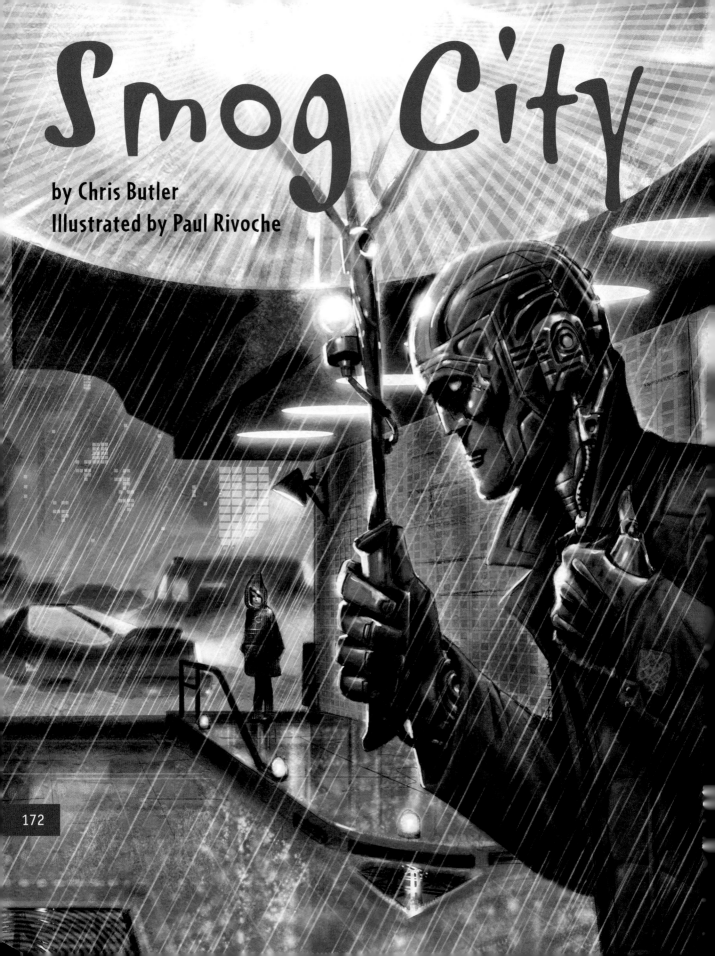

Smog City

by Chris Butler

Illustrated by Paul Rivoche

How can the environment we live in affect our health?

I'm standing at the junction of Denman and Davie, watching as a car turns and speeds away. The exhaust coughs out a cloud of thick, dark smoke that billows and curls in the air. It's another visitor. They come here in their cars and foul up the air some more. I lean forward and breathe in deeply. When you're hungry, nothing tastes as good as the emissions from a diesel engine. The particles go deep inside my lungs, where the acid lining melts them.

There's a bulletin out for a missing 10-year-old girl named Emily, so I'm walking the streets looking for her. Her family lives out near Whistler Mountain, but they came into the city this morning. The girl went missing sometime around 1:30 p.m. It's now 3:30 p.m., and her parents are frantic with worry.

Typical of Vancouver, it's starting to rain. The few people on the streets are scattering, seeking shelter in the shops and restaurants. Only machines live in the city now. Metal men like me. Humans can visit once in a while—once a month is considered safe—but they can't live here anymore. The acid rain would peel their skin off and the smog would rot out their lungs.

I take my umbrella from my pocket, open it up, and listen as the raindrops bounce noisily off the acid-resistant shelter. As I'm pulling my coat tightly around myself, I spot her—a lone figure on the other side of the crossing, almost hidden by the sheets of rain. Could this be the girl? When the traffic lights change she runs across, feet splashing in the pooling water.

> **READ LIKE A WRITER**
> What details does the writer use to show us that this is a science fiction story?

173

"Wait!" I call, but she runs straight past me, down toward the beach. I hear her coughing, and think that she shouldn't be out of bed, never mind out in this downpour. I follow her, trying to keep the umbrella over me, my raincoat whipping in the wind. I stop suddenly where the pavement merges with the sand.

"Hello!" I shout, trying to lift my voice above the wind and rain. I'm reluctant to go out onto the sand because it plays havoc with my joints.

The girl turns toward me, her small face peering out from the hood of her coat. I match the image against the missing person report, and confirm that she is the one. I send a telepathic report to headquarters indicating that I have found her.

She coughs again, a deep wheezing sound, and then turns back toward the ocean. I take a few cautious steps toward her and call out, "You know, your parents are looking for you!"

"I got lost," she says, "but I recognize this place." Her voice is muffled by the hood of her coat and by the rain, but my hearing is excellent. She turns around, and I see her pale face as she starts to walk back toward me. "I just so wanted to see the ocean," she says. "And my parents . . . ." Then she stumbles and falls down into the sand.

I run to her and kneel down, holding the umbrella to shelter her. Her breath is less than a shallow wheeze now. I listen carefully to the air travelling in and out of her body, and can tell that her lungs are raw with infection. "Are you asthmatic?" I ask.

She nods. "I haven't been to the city in years because it only makes me worse," she says. "We live up in the mountains where the air is clearer, but even there it is getting worse. I pleaded with Mom and Dad to let me come here today. I miss it so."

175

People do still come to the city, still driving in their cars, spewing carbon monoxide, oxides of nitrogen, volatile organic compounds, and particulates into the air. But when they get here they stay indoors, in the malls, where the air is purified. Not many people come down to the beach anymore. I've been told that it is still beautiful, even now, with the waves breaking against the shore, but I'm no judge of that.

"Help is on the way," I tell the girl, and we wait together. Then I hear an ambulance and a police car arriving. Her parents get out of the car and rush toward us.

"I'm Emily," she tells me, knowing that she only has moments before her trip to the beach will come to an end. "Thanks for helping me, mister."

"Yes, thank you," her father says, but he does not look at me. Emily's mother is hugging her as they climb into the ambulance. I hear the woman say to her husband, "We have to move farther north—and very soon." Her husband agrees. "I'm sure we can still sell the house," he says.

I sit down on one of the gnarled and twisted logs scattered on the beach. It creaks and a piece of the bark breaks off and falls into the sand. I look out across the bay. The rain has stopped, and somewhere above the dark rain clouds I see a hint of the Sun. That's all we ever see of it now. I think of Emily and hope that she will be okay. I liked the way she called me "mister." Like I was one of them, a real person.

I stand up and hobble back to the pavement, feeling the sand in my knee. I have reached the end of my shift, so I figure I'll head over to the repair cell, where they'll fix me up.

The rain has cleared the air a little. But this is not such a good thing for a hungry metal man. Still, it will soon be rush hour, when the good folk get back into their cars and head home to the northern hills.

I take a walk up toward the busier streets, hoping to find some fresh smog for dinner.

DIG DEEPER ·······················

1. Make a story map that shows the setting, characters, and events of the story.

2. In a small group, discuss other ways that the environment can affect our body systems. List ideas on a chart.

Setting	Main Characters
Beginning	
Events	

Connect and Share

Now it's your turn to share what you've learned about body systems. Prepare a news report about a body organ or system.

Plan Your News Report

- Choose an interesting topic about a body organ or system you have learned about.
- List some interesting facts about it to share with your family.
- Write a short news item about the topic as if you were a TV news reporter.

Share with Your Family

- Present your news item to your family.
- Together find at least two more facts to add to your item.
- Share your item with a partner or group at school.

TIPS FOR A NEWS ITEM

- Have a "lead" that tells the most interesting part.
- Keep it short—no more than 45 seconds.
- Practise sounding very excited about your news item.

Spotlight on **Learning**

Collect

- Gather your notebooks, your writing, and your projects from this unit.

Talk and reflect

Work with a partner.

- Together, read the Learning Goals on page 120.

- Talk about how well you met these goals.

- Look through your work for evidence.

My choices	I want this in my portfolio because...

Select

- Choose two pieces of work that show how you achieved the Learning Goals. (The same piece of work can show more than one goal.)

Tell about your choices

- Tell what each piece shows about your learning.

Reflect

- What have you learned about how science topics are researched and presented to others?

- How has your learning about body systems changed your thinking about healthy living?

179

Acknowledgements

Permission to reprint copyrighted material is gratefully acknowledged. Every effort has been made to trace ownership of all copyrighted material and to secure permission from copyright holders. In the event of any questions arising as to the use of any material, we will be pleased to make the necessary corrections in future printings.

Student Book

Photographs

2–3 Terry Vine/Stone/Getty Images; **6 t** © Digital Vision/Getty Images, **b** © Andrew Rubtsov/Alamy; **7** Juan Manuel Silva/A.G.E. Foto Stock/First Light; **8 l–r** Cover from *The Kids Book of Great Canadians* illustrated by John Mantha used by permission of Kids Can Press. Cover illustration © John Mantha, Historica Web page used with permission of Historica, www.histori.ca., Photo of David Suzuki used with permission of CBC Design Library, Still Photo Collection, Mei Yu Art Web page used with permission of Mei Yu, www.meiyuart.com, "The Wide World of Tim Berners-Lee" used with permission of *YES Mag*, www.yesmag.ca; **9** Ray Boudreau; **iv, 10** Courtesy of Todd Wong, www.gunghaggisfatchoy.com; **11** www.tempestphoto.com; **iv, 12–13** Courtesy of Wanda Robson, Nova Scotia; **14** Courtesy of Erica Samms-Hurley; **15** Courtesy of Rideau Hall (Issa Paré); **16 t** Ray Boudreau, **b** PhotoObjects.net/Jupiter Images; **17** Ray Boudreau; **18** Last Asahi team, 1941. Columbia Studio. Courtesy of Reggie Yasui; **19 sidebar** Brand X/Jupiter Images, **b** Courtesy of Pat Adachi; **20** Library and Archives Canada/C-046355; **v, 21 tl** Comstock/ Jupiter Images, **middle l** Comstock/Jupiter Images, **v, tr** Brand X/ Jupiter Images; **22** Courtesy of Pat Adachi; **23–24** Courtesy of Free The Children, www.freethechildren.com; **26–27** Courtesy of Free The Children, www.freethechildren.com; **v, 28–29** © Photo by Mike Grandmaison. Used with permission of Arts City Inc. Artist: Katharina Stieffenhofer. Youth participants from Art City and Winnipeg high schools and collegiate institutes. Supported by the City of Winnipeg. www.themuralsofwinnipeg.com; **30–31** © Photo by Mike Grandmaison. Used with permission of Manitoba Housing Authority. Painted by: Chandler McLeod; www.themuralsofwinnipeg.com; **32–33** Installation

135 Ray Boudreau; **136 t** Ablestock/Jupiter Images, **middle** Laurence Monneret/Stone/Getty Images; **ix, 138** BrandX/Jupiter Images; **139 tr** Anna Summa/Taxi/Getty Images; **ix, 141** Pasieka/Science Photo Library; **142** Hank Morgan/ Science Photo Library; **143 t** Photo courtesy of L-1 Identity Solutions, Inc., **b** James King-Holmes/Science Photo Library; **144 tl** Geoff Tompkinson/Science Photo Library, **b** James King-Holmes/Science Photo Library; **145 t** Photo courtesy of L-1 Identity Solutions, Inc., **b** Mauro Fermariello/Photo Researchers, Inc.; **152** Ray Boudreau; **157 t** Comstock/Jupiter Images, **b** M. Kulyk/Photo Researchers, Inc.; **158–159** © Dennis Kunkel/Phototake; **160** Steve Gschmeissner/Photo Researchers, Inc.; **161 bl** © Shutterstock; **ix, 162 t and b** PhotoObjects/ Jupiter Images; **163 middle** Comstock/Jupiter Images; **164 t** Olivier Ribardiere/Taxi/Getty Image, **b** BananaStock/Jupiter Images; **166 t** Paul Tearle/Stockbyte/Getty Images, **b** Used with permission of George Brown College; **167 tl** Thinkstock/Jupiter Images, **background** BrandX/Jupiter Images; **168** Ryan McVay/Stone/Getty Images; **178** © Brand X/Alamy; **179** Creatas/Jupiter Images

Illustrations

iv, 4–5 Laurie Lafrance; **7, 25** Deborah Crowle Art; **35** Laurie Lafrance; **v, 40–45** © Caroline Magerl; **v, 46–59** © Janice Lee Porter; **62–63** Kurt Varg/Stock Illustration Source/VEER; **vi, 66–67** Stephanie Power; **vi, 70–75** Ron Dollekamp/Three in a Box Inc; **78–81** Ben Shannon; **85–89** Ramón Pérez, colour assist by Andy Bélanger; **90–91** Christopher Hutsul; **92–96** Ben Shannon; **103** Anne MacInnes; **vii, 104–109** © Kevin Hawkes; **viii, 122–125** Carl Wiens; **viii, 128** Bo Veisland/Photo Researchers Inc.; **130** 3D4Medical.com/Getty Images; **viii, 132** 3D4Medical.com/Getty Images; **137, 139–140** Jeff Dixon; **146–151** Diane Dawson Hearn; **153** Anne MacInnes; **154–156** © Lane Smith; **161–163** Dave Whamond/Three in a Box Inc; **165** Deborah Crowle Art; **ix, 169–171** Martin Gagnon; **172–177** Paul Rivoche

Text

18–22 "For the Love of the Game" by the Canadian Baseball Hall of Fame and Museum; **38–39** "The Language of Friendship": This article first appeared in *Discovery Girls Magazine*, Vol. 5, no. 5 (October/ November 2005). Reprinted with permission of Discovery Girls, Inc.; **40–45** "My Gran's Different," extract from *MY GRAN'S DIFFERENT* by Sue Lawson and Caroline Magerl courtesy of Lothian Children's Books,

Shared Reading Posters

Photographs

Illustrations